J.

CHUCKLES FROM CHILDREN

Jackie:

Best thoughts and warm wishes
From our house to yours

Mary Winkler

CHUCKLES FROM CHILDREN

Mary Winkler

VANTAGE PRESS
New York

FIRST EDITION

Published by Vantage Press, Inc.
516 West 34th Street, New York, New York 10001

Manufactured in the United States of America
ISBN: 0-533-11497-7

Library of Congress Catalog Card No.: 95-90207

0 9 8 7 6 5 4 3 2

Preface

I have found that children of all ages have their own way of looking at and handling different situations in life. Like a fresh breeze, they have an innocent and honest way of expressing themselves . . . the topic of this book, *Chuckles from Children*, which is a conglomeration of over five hundred *true* stories!

Sitting around our kitchen table, sharing coffee with some friends, is how this book got started. I shared the story of our five-year-old granddaughter's surprised reactions to the leak in the old water flume and was told the story of the girl and the hobo. Then, another friend shared the story of little Matthew thinking that the small dog growling at him was *purring!* One story led to another, and another, etc., etc. Knowing these stories had actually happened lent something special to each story as it was being related.

When, after a few days had gone by, I thought about those stories, I would break out laughing anew. I decided I would start collecting such true stories and make a book of them.

I want to thank our family and friends and the many strangers for their personal stories, making *Chuckles from Children* such a happy possibility.

God bless each and every one of you.

A little three-year-old girl (I'll call her Annie) would never pick her blankets up off the floor. Her mother was trying very hard to teach Annie to keep them picked up. One day, Annie's mother went into little Annie's bedroom, and (sure enough) there was Annie standing on a blanket on the floor. Her mother immediately started scolding Annie about it. "Annie, I've been teaching you to keep your blankets on your bed. Now, WHY is that blanket on the floor?"

Putting her tiny hands on her little hips, Annie looked up at her mother and, while defiantly shaking her head, answered, "WELL! I'm teaching IT to be a RUG!"

———————

When little three-year-old Deseria was given a present of some daintily ruffled red panties, Deseria would put them on and, while happily wiggling her little bottom end, proudly tell everyone, "THESE are my SEXY panties!"

———————

Most of the time (since infancy) little three-year-old Chris and his mommy had lived with Chris's beloved grandma. One day, a short time after Chris and his mother had moved into a home of their own, Chris's mother dialed his grandma's phone number. When his grandmother answered, Chris's mother just handed the telephone over to Chris. Soon came the very, very tearful voice of little Chris, saying, "Grandma, I'm just a a-whinin' and a-bawlin' to come to YOUR house!"

———————

A group of young boys in the front pew were being addressed by the minister, who was asking each one in turn, "What has the Lord done for you?"

The last little boy (just loaded with freckles) answered, "He almost RUINT me!"

It has long been my standard remark when I first meet a very young girl and/or very young boy: "Are you married?" Their reaction is almost always the same: first the gasp, then the slight delay (to make SURE they had heard my question right), and then with a twinkle in their eyes and a bashful smile, they inform me, "Noooo! I'm only [their age] old!"

However, one day there was just a bit more to the story. I had asked our new five-year-old neighbor girl if SHE was married. After the usual cute little show had taken place, I was informed by the little girl's grandmother that they had gone to a wedding the day before in which her granddaughter had been the flower girl. She asked, "Grandma, will the other people here at the wedding think I am the bride?"

While riding with his mother at Christmastime, five-year-old Shawn had spotted a small evergreen tree growing along the road. Since Shawn hadn't seen any decorations on the little tree, he sadly told his mother, "That poor little tree doesn't have any Christmas!"

Little three-year-old Daniel was snuggled up on the daven-port with Terrie and Tim. They were all watching a television show in which some men were trying to rescue some prisoners of war. Little Daniel was watching closely, very intent on all of the action, when Tim asked, "Well, Daniel, aren't you going to help those guys?"

Daniel quickly replied, "I can't! I can't! I can't get into the TV anymore!"

Which brings to mind a similar story about a young boy who had received a BB gun from his parents. It seems this little guy was watching a cowboy story on TV and was intently observing all of the gunplay that was taking place. He decided to help his hero. He raised the barrel of his BB gun and shot . . . killing the TV set DEAD!

One day, pretty little three-year-old Beth was busy putting her six dolls to bed. With great care, she fixed their beds. Then, in turn, she undressed each doll and put its pajamas on before tucking it into its bed . . . doll number 1, number 2, 3, 4, 5, and 6. Beth then lay down beside them. She lay there for about five minutes (almost going to sleep) before she got back up. Quickly she shook her head and stated, "Kids, kids, kids! I can't sleep a wink!"

At about four and a one-half years of age, little Mary was quite a copycat, repeating everything she had heard someone else say. It wasn't very nice of her, and she became quite a thorn in just EVERYONE'S side. Mary's family tried everything they could think of to get her to stop repeating what she heard others say, but nothing worked; she simply wouldn't stop.

One morning Mary overheard her older sister, Thelma, telling her friend, "I don't feel very good, Dodie. I have a headache."

So, Mary said, "I don't feel very good, Dodie. I have a headache."

Thelma said, "And my eyes burn."

And Mary said, "And my eyes burn."

Dodie said, "My throat is raw."

And Mary said, "My throat is raw."

Thelma said, "My arm hurts."

And Mary said, "My arm hurts."

Dodie said, "My stomach is upset."

3

And Mary said, "My stomach is upset."
Thelma said, "My back aches."
And Mary said, "My back aches."
Dodie said, "My knees hurt."
And Mary said, "My knees hurt."
Thelma said, "My big toe even hurts."
And Mary said, "My big toe even hurts."

Then, in one big, long breath, Dodie said, "My head aches; my eyes burn; my throat is raw; my stomach is upset; my back aches; my arm hurts; my knees hurt; why, my big toe even hurts!"

Dodie and Thelma were curious as to how their little echo would handle SO much in such a short time.

Little Mary thought about it for a few seconds before saying, "Gee, Dodie, you DO feel bad!"

Little five-year-old Mary and her seven-year-old brother, Bob, were spending the summer with their grandmother, who lived next door to a lady known to them as Mrs. Whitaker. Mrs. Whitaker's house was separated from their grandmother's house by a very tall fence, which continued on down the hill behind their houses, thus separating their backyards as well.

At one time, the two ladies had been friends. However, that friendship had broken up, as their grandmother and Mrs. Whitaker did not get along with each other (didn't even try). In fact, every time their grandmother would go outside to dump her dirty dishwater, she would toss it over the tall fence with the comment: "I hope 'SHE' is over there and gets wet!"

One day little Mary and Bob were playing on the front porch. Little Mary was jumping rope while keeping time to the recital of a little poem (which she was calling out at the top of her voice):

"Chew tobacco, chew tobacco
Spit—spit—Spit. . . .
Old Lady Whitaker
Thinks SHE'S IT!"

In a short while, a police car pulled up in front of their house and while one of the two policemen went in to talk to their grandmother, little Mary and her brother, Bob, visited with the other policeman.

During children's communion (where children come to the altar for blessing with a hand on the head rather than blessing with bread and wine) one little five-year-old boy let it be known that, "I don't like your hand on MY head; just give ME some of that bread!"

Before you read the following story, please keep in mind, in the private family life of a military family (right from the start) the children are trained to answer questions with a proper: "Yes, sir!"; "No, sir!"; "Thank you"; "No, thank you"; etc., etc. . . .

A lieutenant colonel in the army engineers had invited a newly arrived lieutenant and his family to his home for dinner. During the dinner, the lieutenant colonel's ten-year-old son, David, asked to be excused to go outside and play. David was excused and was playing outside when his father (the lieutenant colonel) called to him, "David, would you like some pie for desert?"

David quickly answered, "No!"

Now, not getting the expected CORRECT answer of: "No, thank you," David's father asked, "David, no WHAT?"

David answered, "No PIE!"

Ten-year-old Joanne was going through her mother's purse and decided to rummage through her wallet also. On examining her driver's license, Joanne turned to her mother and asked, "Mom, why did you get an F in sex?"

The song "Washed in the Blood of the Lord" being sung at a

baptism made one young Texan lad wonder, "Why don't they come up red?"

After being told about the fight on the playground, naturally, both of the fighters (I'll call them Pete and Joe) were kept after school so they could be talked to. When they were asked what their problem was and who had started the fight, neither one of the boys would say anything. Finally, as a last resort, the teacher made the comment: "I don't know what I am going to tell your parents, boys. This is a small town, and I've known BOTH of your families for years. I just don't know how to explain your conduct to them. Just WHY were you fighting like that?"

Pete said, "Joe started the fight. He hit me first!"

Joe quickly responded, "Well, Pete called me an 'A'-HOLE!"

Raising her eyebrows, the teacher then said, "Why, Pete! Just what will your folks say when I tell them this?"

"Oh they won't mind," Pete nonchalantly replied. "They call each other that all the time, at home!"

No doubt about it, the horror stories about cannibals eating people shown on the movie screens and on television ARE pretty scary to children. Not too much may be thought about it by grown-ups, but the stories DO make an impression on children, as the following anecdote points out.

One day, while a family was on a trip up in Canada, a Canadian farmer was spotted by the family and the remark was made: "Now, THERE is a real, live native Canadian farmer!"

The little six-year-old girl (hanging onto the back of the driver's seat) got even closer to her dad, asking in a really scared voice, "He [the Canadian farmer] won't EAT us, will he, Daddy?"

At the age of six and one-half years, Brian, together with his aunt and his cousin, went on a tour of a fire station. The fireman was explaining a hypothetical situation. "Now, we know this house is on fire," he said. "We don't know which room the fire

6

is in. You put your hand up against a closed door and it's hot, so you know the fire is burning on the other side." Turning to the boys, he asked, "Then, what do you do?"

Brian quickly answered, "I'd take MY hand off that hot door!"

When six-year-old Sherri Lynn had trouble with ten-year-old Larry pulling her curls, Sherri Lynn talked to her grandmother about it. Her grandmother said, "Now, Sherri, don't you try to hit him; he's bigger than you. And don't scratch him with your fingernails. Just kick him. . . . THAT should keep him away!"

One day, Sherri Lynn's first-grade teacher called Sherri's grandmother down to the school to discuss a fight that little Sherri had been involved in on the school grounds. With her eyes full of tears, Sherri Lynn said, "I don't know WHY I'm in trouble, Grandma. I did just like you told me. I didn't hit him, and I didn't scratch him. . . . I KICKED him!"

For most of their married life, this elderly couple had not had a very good bed. One day, their six-year-old grandson, Matthew, was visiting, and while watching his grandfather making up their bed, little Matthew said, "Gee whiz, Grandpa, you don't have a very good bed!"

His grandfather started to explain, rather nervously, "That's right, Matthew. We have just never gotten around to buying us a decent bed."

Matthew agreed, then confidently added, "Why, Grandpa, they have better beds [than yours] down at Saint Vincent de Paul's!"

While at the summer church camp, the children were asked the question: "If you could live in any other time period, which would you choose?"

A little seven-year-old girl answered, "I would choose the

7

time of the Crusades, because, first, I love Jesus . . . and next, because I like to travel."

Every time little Elsie needed to be punished, her dad would do so by switching her legs, which resulted in red streaks on her legs (which remained for a time). Naturally, Elsie noticed these red streaks. Now, her grandmother was spending some time with the family and while the woman was in the process of changing her heavy cotton stockings, little two-and-a-half year-old Elsie saw her grandmother's varicose veins. She lovingly patted her grandmother's legs and asked, "My daddy been switchin' you, too, Grandma?"

One night, little Terry's daddy took two-year-old Terry outside to see the brilliant display of stars. They stood outside, with little Terry standing on some boards and boxes, for quite some time, enjoying the view. The following day, little Terry kept trying to stand on a small ladderlike stool while looking up at the kitchen ceiling. When his mother asked him what he was doing, Terry said, "I'm trying to see the SHARS!"

For some reason of her own, two-year-old Emily was furiously resisting being potty-trained. She was going to be spending some days in a day-care center, so there was a deeper concern felt for correcting the problem quickly. One day Emily's daddy just wasn't going to give up so easily and kept on insisting (both manually AND verbally) that little Emily stay on the toilet. Emily was just as insistent that she was NOT going to, saying, "You're making me mad, Dad! Go away!"

When the little two-year-old boy was playing outside in the winter snow, his mother (wanting him to come in) commented, "Oh, honey! Your little hands are just frozen!"

"That's right, Mommy, and so are my little mittens!"

Little Rick had received a box of Magic Markers for his fourth birthday. Although Rick was a very quiet little boy (most of the time), he was SO proud of the Magic Markers, every time someone came to visit Rick would show the visitor his present while proudly explaining, "THESE are MAGIC MARKERS!"

Rick's little two-year-old brother, David, would watch Rick go through this routine, and after about the sixth person had been shown and told and Rick had gone off to play, David walked over to the lady and, with a solemn look upon his face, said in a matter-of-fact tone of voice, "Really, they aren't magic. Rick just THINKS they are!"

A Sunday school class was being taught about the sun, moon, stars, and Earth. In order to emphasize the lesson, they colored pictures that Cindy had drawn. Later, in church, a little four-year-old boy was showing a lady what his pictures looked like and the lady said, "Oh, that's nice. And, do you know who made the sun, moon, stars, and Earth?"

The little boy quickly replied, "Sure! Cindy made them!"

And another little four-year-old boy (who was used to but did not like, his mother working all of the time) was asked, "What are you going to be when you grow up?"

He answered, "I am going to be a MOM so I can stay home and watch TV all the time!"

Gene's daughter was going to college in Moscow, Idaho, and Gene was going to go down to visit her there. Since he had planned on taking her out to dinner, they were to meet in a restaurant near the college. As Gene had never been in that particular part of Moscow before, his daughter had given him directions (going through the campus, of course) to the restaurant where they were to meet. While he was driving along he was visiting with his friend who was in the seat beside him. All of a sudden, it dawned on him that, just maybe, he should have been paying more attention to WHERE he was driving! He thought that he might have missed a turn somewhere. Aloud, he said, "HEY! I had better pay more attention, here. . . . We just MIGHT be lost!"

His little three-and-a-half-year-old grandson, Nathaniel, sitting in the backseat, immediately started looking out the car windows, then said, "No, we're not lost, Grandpa. We're STILL in Moscow!"

———————————

At three years of age, Jeannie had broken her leg. Naturally, she had to spend a long time with her leg in a cast (so the bone could heal properly). One day, little Jeannie was feeling extra blue and asked, "Daddy, if you will just take me fishing, I promise I'll sit in the car!"

———————————

While driving into Spokane one day, Al and his three-year-old son, Tim, got into a fight. Little Tim was still mad at his dad when they went by a used-car lot with all the trade-in advertisements. Tim's mother asked, "Should we trade Daddy off?"

To which Tim quickly answered, "YES, and let's get a black one!"

———————————

"What Is Your Nationality" was the topic being discussed by the first-grade class when six-year-old Glenn proudly claimed to be English, Irish, and dachshund!

———————————

It was Casey's sixth birthday. Since it was a special day, Rich asked Casey and his two older brothers if they would like to go for a ride in Rich's restored 1958 Cadillac. Naturally, they all wanted to, so Rich had the three boys sit in the backseat, closed the door, then got in behind the wheel, closed his door, and put a cigar in his mouth before starting the motor. They left the driveway before Rich lit his cigar. After a VERY short time, Casey asked, "Hey, Rich, would you mind putting that thing out? I just brushed my teeth!"

———————————

A little first-grade boy was happily sharing the news of the new baby at his house with his teacher and classmates, adding, "Mama's not gonna have no more babies. She had her TONSILS tied!"

———————————

"Clouds are fun! They can be ANYTHING I want them to be . . . witches, horses, islands in a blue sea, mountains, or baby angels. But Daddy says clouds are vaporated moy-sure, whatever THAT means!"

———————————

Les was in the process of remodeling their home, doing the work himself. While working on replacing the roof, he happened to step on a loose rafter, causing him to fall to the cement below and break his arm. His wife, Delores, and their two-year-old daughter, Barbara, were standing by the kitchen door and saw all of this take place. Little Barbara asked, "Daddy! Why didn't you use the ladder?"

———————————

While watching his new baby sister suckling at her mother's breast, a two-year-old boy said, "Them's GOOD, Sissy. Them's 2 percent."

———————————

Little two-year-old Annie would help check for traffic at the intersections. She would look both ways, and when there were no cars, she would call out, "ALL QUEER!"

When his daddy has a really bad headache, two-year-old Trevor's advice is: "Daddy, take two aspirin and come see me in the mornin'!"

Little four-year-old Jesse was telling his mother, "Mom, I don't think I like Bridgett anymore."

Since Bridgett was their baby-sitter, his mother wanted to know what had happened, so she asked, "Why not, Jesse?"

"Well . . . every time Bridgett comes over to baby-sit, she ALWAYS tells me, 'You're gonna get it now, Jesse!' But, Mom, she never tells me what IT is!"

Four-year-old Krista has beautiful big eyes of a very pale blue color. People have often stopped and commented about them, remarking on their unusual color and beauty.

One day the family was seated in the Broken Wheel (one of the local cafés) having dinner. A waitress walked by, stopped, turned around to their table, and asked little Krista, "Where did you get those BEAUTIFUL blue eyes?"

Krista looked up at the waitress and (in a matter-of-fact manner) answered, "From the milkman!"

One day, four-year-old Benjamin was riding with his daddy along a very busy street. (The heavy traffic was moving along at a fast pace.) The car in front of theirs stopped suddenly, causing Benjamin's daddy to apply the brakes rather abruptly, which naturally caused everything to come to a screeching halt. Being pretty upset, he was muttering to himself and calling the other driver some (not very nice) names. Little Benjamin listened, quietly, for a while, then asked, "Why did you do that, Daddy? If you would be patient and wait, that car will move!"

Members of the Church of Latter Day Saints are very strongly advised not to abuse their bodies with substances such as alcohol, nicotine, or other harmful drugs.

One day, while waiting in an airport terminal, a little five-year-old Mormon girl saw a man sitting and smoking a cigarette. She walked over to him and said, "You should NOT be smoking that."

"Oh, yeah? WHO says so?" the man asked sarcastically.

To which the little girl quickly replied, "Smokey the Bear and Holy the Ghost!"

The kids and their families had come home for Thanksgiving. Grandpa decided to give the ladies a chance to prepare dinner and put it on the table while he took his four little grandsons upstairs to play hide-and-go-seek. The room Grandpa chose to hide in had a large portable clothes closet, upon which he climbed, lying down on top. The boys looked and looked and looked but just couldn't find him anywhere. Finally, they gathered around the end of the clothes closet, and little five-year-old Chris told the others, "Fellas, I don't know WHERE Grandpa could be hiding. We have looked EVERYWHERE for him and can't find him. But . . . we must be close! I can SMELL him!"

Upon finding some new baby kittens behind their garage, some boys were trying to convince their mother, "The neighbor's cat laid some kittens JUST FOR US!"

Two brothers, eight-year-old Carl and six-year-old Tony, had gotten permission to go visit their friend Gilbert for a couple of hours. It was getting close to dark and the boys weren't home, so their mother and dad were becoming worried. However, a short time later, the boys came in and were excitedly telling about their going to the circus! That, by watering the animals, they got in "free" to see the circus.

Their father asked, "Carl, you KNOW that you didn't have permission to go to the circus?"

Looking down at his feet, Carl answered, "I know, Dad."

His father continued, "And, Tony, YOU knew that you shouldn't have gone, too. Why did you go?"

Tony quickly answered, "OH! I couldn't let Carl go by himself! I had to go and look after Carl!"

A discussion was taking place about one of seven-year-old Trina's older cousins getting a summer job delivering newspapers—about the responsibility, the being tied down, the being expected to deliver even if you WERE tired (or wanted to go somewhere special). The amount of money that he was going to make, as well as WHAT he was going to do with it, was also brought up.

Little Trina, who was spending the summer there with relatives, was asked by her grandmother, "Trina, why don't you get a job delivering newspapers, too?"

"Why, Grandma," she said, "I've got PEOPLE to visit!"

"Men have beards and women don't," Mom explains.

Christi wants to know, "Why not? Did God make a mistake?"

The parents of five-year-old Benjamin had been talking to their friend Sheila about making out their will. Later, during a father-to-son discussion with little Benjamin, his dad asked, "Ben, do you know what a 'will' is?"

Benjamin answered, "Yes."

Then Benjamin's dad said, "I want you to tell me, in your own words, what a 'will' is."

Little Benjamin proudly told his daddy, "A WILL is what holds the tire. And when the tire goes flat, you have to remove the WILL before you can mend the tire so you can put air in it again."

14

After having eaten lunch with them, Grandpa (a logger) had decided that it was okay for Grandma and their little five-year-old granddaughter, Serenity, to walk back with him close to where he had been sawing logs. Little Serenity went ahead, skipping up the road, undoubtedly full of vim, vinegar, and curiosity. In a VERY short time, she came running back down the road as fast as she could run, her face ashen white. She was calling, excitedly, "Grandpa, Grandma! Grandpa, Grandma, something's wrong! Something's wrong!" When asked what was the matter, Serenity answered in a quivering voice, "It's raining the wrong way—it's raining upside-down!" There was a leak in the old water flume that was buried along the road and water was shooting up at least five feet into the air!

Little three-year-old Ray's daddy had always worn a mustache. One day he decided to shave it off and went into the bathroom and did just that. Afterward he went out into the hallway, bumping into little Ray there. Ray looked up at his daddy (without his mustache) and, not recognizing him, ran down the hallway in search of his mother screaming, "Mommy! Mommy! There's a YUCKY man in the house!"

While at a local drive-in, the man had just placed an order of hamburgers and french fries for the family. "And, nothing on one of the burgers," he said, speaking for his three-year-old daughter.

The little girl quickly said, "Oh, Daddy! I want a BUN on MY hamburger!"

The Singer Sewing Machine Company's maintenance man had gone to a house for in-home repair service. He was sitting at the sewing machine while a little boy, approximately three years old, was standing off to the side, watching everything the man did. The little boy's busy mother came into the room, and the little boy asked, "Who's that man?"

His mother answered, "That's the Singer man."

The boy walked back over to the Singer man, stood still for a few minutes (just looking at him), then all of a sudden blurted out, "Sing something, Singer man!"

Rod was growing up (an eighth-grader!) and both of his parents who were teachers, although at another school, were kept informed on Rod's grades, behavior, and achievements by his teachers. One day, one of Rod's teachers reported, "Rod COULD and SHOULD be doing better in school."

That evening at the dinner table, Rod's dad asked, "How was your day at school, Son?"

Rod answered, "Just fine, Dad."

His dad asked, "Are you SURE, Son?"

To which Rod answered, "Sure."

His dad took a deep breath and (trying one more time to get Rod to admit that he hadn't been doing his best at school) said, "You know, Son, your mother and I know EVERYTHING there is to know about you, don't you?"

Rod cocked his head to one side and (with a mischievous grin) asked, "Do I have hair under my arms, Dad?"

Charlie's mother was convinced that Jesus might pose as a hobo just to test people's generosity, so she brought her family up keeping this thought in mind, and they NEVER refused to feed a hobo. Consequently, their house (which was close to the railroad tracks) had been marked by the hoboes as an easy place to get a free meal.

One day, a hobo came to their door asking for something to eat and offered to split some wood for the meal. When Charlie's eleven-year-old daughter took the papersack of food out to the hobo, she gave it to him and quickly came back to the house. While pinching her nose between her fingers, she said, "Wheeeooh! If THAT is Jesus, he had better stop walking ON the water and get down IN it!"

———————

One day, one of seven-year-old Jesse's classmates was giving the teacher a terrible time. It seems the boy was doing anything and everything naughty he could think of, and the teacher was right on his case with each episode. Then, the boy pulled something else, for which the teacher was naturally "chewing him out," when Jesse raised his hand, saying to the teacher, "That little boy has had a bad day already, so you shouldn't be so rough on him!"

———————

A little neighbor girl had stopped by to visit her elderly neighbors. On her way into their yard, she stopped and got their newspaper from the paper box and brought it to her neighbor Pat. Pat had been visiting with his friend Harry. Harry (teasingly) said, "Pat, I don't know about your paper girl. Did you know that she doesn't even have any front teeth?"

"No front teeth? I don't know about this," Pat said. "Maybe we shouldn't let a girl with no front teeth be our paper girl!"

To which the little girl quickly retorted, "I'm NOT a PAPER girl. I'm REAL!"

———————

Scott was learning about the planets at the Pacific Science Center. His mother said, "See, Scott, there's Mercury, Venus, Earth, Mars, Jupiter, Saturn—"

"But, Mom . . . where's Texas?"

———————

Sunday school had just gotten over, and the minister was making the church announcements. After the final one, he asked, "Are there any more announcements to be made?"

His little five-year-old daughter, Mable, stood up from the front row and said, "Yes, Daddy. I have some NEW SHOES!"

One day, while five-year-old Chad was riding with his dad around Medical Lake, little Chad saw some ducks out on the water and asked, "What kind of birds are those, Daddy?"

His dad answered, "Those are wild ducks."

Later, they passed a sign along the highway, and Chad asked, "Daddy, what does that sign say?"

His dad answered, "Medical Lake."

Little Chad was thoughtful for a minute or two, then, with a serious look on his face, asked, "Daddy, do they have wild doctors here, too?"

A grandmother had just taken her homemade rhubarb pie from the oven. She found out later that she had forgotten to put the sugar in the pie. When her five-year-old granddaughter stopped in to visit, she accepted the offer of a piece of the warm rhubarb pie, took her first bite and after a few minutes, with her face still all puckered up, said, "Gee, Grandma, you sure do make good BARBED-WIRE pie!"

Millie was the janitor of a small school for quite a number of years and enjoyed a one-on-one type friendship with many of the students there. One of these students, a twelve-year old boy I'll call James, seemed to be in a conflict most of the time. Not only did he have trouble with his schoolwork and with his teachers, but also in getting along with the other students.He was almost ALWAYS in an argument or a fight with someone!

Millie had watched all of this taking place, and she wanted James to know that SHE was his friend; she thought by being his friend, maybe she could help him to solve some of his disagreements without fighting. So, with this thought in mind, one day Millie told him, "James, don't let those other kids knock you around so much. Just give me a call and I'll help you out."

In a very short time after walking off, she heard a frantic

call from James: "MILLIE! Get your fat a—— back here and help me knock h—— out of these G——D—— kids!"

When Harry and Mary came in from work one night, it was to a big surprise. Their son, Butch, and two of his friends had baked (and frosted with chocolate icing) a big chocolate cake for Mary's birthday!

Upon receiving a birthday card and the cake, Mary said, "Oh, this is so very nice of you boys! I thank you very much. However, there goes my diet, because THIS is my favorite kind of cake!"

Instantly she was informed that, "THIS chocolate cake is NOT fattening! IT'S made with EX-LAX!"

Doris, a young neighbor girl, was visiting with Dino one warm summer day. A fly was buzzing around the kitchen, giving Dino and his young friend a bad time. Dino had tried, many times, to swat the fly, but somehow it managed to evade the swatter. While sitting there in the kitchen, seven-year-old Doris noticed a hole in Dino's screen door and said, "Dino, do you know that you have a hole in the bottom part of your screen door?"

Jokingly Dino answered, "Oh, I have that hole there so the flies can get back outside and I don't have to kill them."

Doris was quiet for a short time while watching a fly crawl around at the top of the screen door. Then, she said, "Dino, I think it would work better if you had the hole at the TOP instead of the bottom!"

School pictures had been taken that day at school. Later, at home, the boys were talking about the different ways the photographers had used to make smiles. They asked eight-year-old Josh to say, "Girl-crazy," and snapped the camera. They asked six-year-old Matthew to say, "Pepsi," and snapped the camera.

Matthew then told about one of the boys in his class who

would just NOT smile. Nothing seemed to work. Then, just out of the blue, the boy said, "My mother has holes in her under-wear!" and then REALLY laughed. So the photographers got a big smile after all!

Little three-year-old Fred's name for robins: "Belly-birds!"

Since their family was spending Christmas with them, Lois and Jim's house was really crowded. Their young grandson, seven-year-old Matthew, had fallen in love with his grandma and grandpa's small dog, old Sammie, wanting to pet her, hug her, and talk to her every chance he got. Now, Sammie was an old dog and she was nervous when around children and would snap, usually at their faces! The grown-ups, being aware of this, could imagine Matthew coming up without a nose! With much effort on their part, they managed to keep Matthew separated from old Sammie . . . UNTIL the last few minutes. While the visitors were preparing to leave and with almost everyone at the door (all talking at the same time), the attention was not on Matthew and old Sammie. All of a sudden, his grandma happened to think about them, and sure enough, there was Matthew hovering over old Sammie, telling her good-bye, with old Sammie all stretched out on the leather ottoman, growling deep in her throat! When Matthew was told to back away, Matthew said, "It's okay, Grandma. Sammie isn't mad at me; she's PURRIN'!"

There was no doubt about it (his mother had the facts from his second-grade teacher)—this seven-year-old boy wasn't get-ting his work finished and turned in on time. When his mother asked, "Why aren't you doing your schoolwork and getting it turned in on time, Son?" the boy thought for a few seconds, then calmly said, "Well, Mom, do you want GOOD work or do you want FAST work?"

While watching a banana being peeled, little two-year-old Allen said, "It's getting its pajamas off!"

———————

Freda's three-year-old daughter, Joy, was learning about God. "God is love, honey," Freda said. "In the beginning, God made Adam and Eve, all the animals, birds, and fish, as well as a place for all to live. And He made you and me."

Little Joy asked, "Well, where IS God, Mommy?"

To which her mother answered, "God is in our heart." Then the conversation was dropped.

About a week later, Freda was frying a chicken for Sunday dinner. She had the pieces floured and waiting to be put into the skillet when Joy came over and, pointing to the gizzard and the heart, asked, "What are those, Mommy?"

"This is the gizzard," Freda said, picking it up and putting it in the skillet. "And this is the heart." She picked up the heart to put into the skillet, too.

With a horrified look on her face, Joy (VERY emphatically) cried out, "MOMMY! Don't cook GOD!"

———————

Thelma and Stanch (Thelma's bald-headed husband) were at our house one evening visiting wih Harry and me. We were all talking and laughing, just having a nice time. Something, however, had been bothering our little three-year-old son, Butch, all evening, and when I went into the kitchen for more coffee, Butch whispered to me, "Mommy, what's wrong with Stanch's head?"

"Well, why don't you ask HIM, Butch?" I asked.

Butch waited for a little while (all the time watching the reflection of the overhead light on Stanch's bald head). Finally, Butch couldn't stand it any longer and went over to stand in front of Stanch, asking, "What's wrong with your head, Stanch? Are you CRACKED?"

———————

For the first six months of their married life, the parents of eight-year-old Josh and six-year-old Matthew had lived in a trailer they had parked in a beautiful (although remote) timbered area of Shoshone County, Idaho.

On a family outing to this same area, the boys' father made the remark, "THIS is where your mother and I lived for the first six months of our married life! In fact, Josh, YOU were conceived while we were living here! Yes, this is where your life first began."

At first, little Matthew didn't have anything to say. He looked all around and, after a few minutes, commented, "Well, I'm sure that God just swooped down, swooshed around a few times, made Josh, and then left!"

One day, eight-year-old Heather was riding with her grandfather in his pickup truck. He had some cracked ribs and was wearing a support band with a Velcro closure. The band had loosened a little bit, so he closed it, catching (and pulling) some of the hair on his chest and causing him to utter a few swearwords!

Later, upon leaving his pickup, he looked back and said, "BOY! What a mess! I'm going to have to clean this pickup out!"

Little Heather looked up at him, and said, "You need to clean your mouth out, TOO, Grandpa!"

About duck hunting, Stormy says, "I don't know WHY they SHOOT the duck. . . . The FALL alone would kill it!"

One day, Patsy had taken her three young nephews up on the mountain behind her house to play games. She told them, "Boys, you go hide, while I close my eyes and count." She was, however, secretly hoping they wouldn't go too far away to hide.

When she turned to look for them, little four-year-old Justin was standing in the tall weeds with the top of his head showing. Patsy called out to him, "Justin, aren't you going to hide?"

At that time, four-year-old Marcus quickly raised his arm while calling out excitedly, "Here I am, Aunt Patsy!"

Then, little three-year-old Keith stood up in the weeds, raising his arms and calling out, "Here I am, TOO!"

Of the three boys, little Justin was the only one that hid and stayed hidden (but with his head showing!).

———————

Marie, a little kindergarten girl, came home from school absolutely heartbroken one day. When she had finally stopped her uncontrollable sobbing, she told her mother about her awful problem. "Mommy, one of the boys in my class loves me, and wants us to get married! And, Mommy, I love him, too . . . BUT I just don't want to leave home yet! OH, Mommy, what am I going to do?"

———————

After being scolded by her aunt for having jumped on her grandmother's bed, little three-year-old Becky quickly told her aunt, "When I'm at Grandma's house, I can do ANYTHING I want to!"

———————

Seven-year-old Chris and his eight-year-old cousin, Brad, were spending the day at Chris's grandfather's house. Although the two boys are cousins, Chris's grandfather is not Brad's grandfather, and this was causing Brad to feel just a little nervous, as he was just a bit scared of the man.

There had been a carton of pop bottles sitting along the wall in the garage where the boys had been playing, and now those bottles were broken. When Chris's grandpa came out, he noticed the broken bottles but didn't say anything. They all climbed into the pickup, with the boys in the back and Grandpa getting into the cab. He turned in the seat and slid the back window open and in a deep voice said, "I see those pop bottles have been broken. Chris, did YOU do it?"

Quickly Chris answered, "No."

Grandpa asked, "Brad, what do YOU know about it?"

In a very scared voice, Brad answered, "I only know ONE thing: I didn't do it."

Grandpa said, "Chris, what do you know about it?"

To which Chris answered, "I don't know nothin'!"

Again, Grandpa asked, "Brad?"

And, again, Brad answered, "I STILL know just ONE thing: I didn't do it!"

So, Grandpa looked at Chris, and Chris asked, "I have a question: will the person that did it get punished when they confess?"

One day, six-year-old Angie and her seven-year-old cousin, Lisa, were at the kitchen table with Angie's mother. Angie asked, "Mommy, why do bears hitchhike?"

To which Lisa quickly retorted, "ANGIE! Those bears aren't HITCHHIKING. . . . They're HY-GER-BATE-IN'!"

At seven years of age, Jack had already had several minor accidents, which, naturally, had left their marks. One day Jack was visiting with his aunt. (She has Alzheimer's, which causes a loss of memory.) Every time his aunt would look at him, she'd notice the marks caused by his accidents and ask, "What on EARTH happened to YOU?"

Jack explained what had happened to him. After about the sixth time his aunt asked him, "What on EARTH happened to YOU?" Jack was running out of patience and answered, "My mom BEAT me!"

On a camping trip to the lake with the family, Dad said, "I won't be able to make pancakes this time, because I don't have all of the stuff!"

But eight-year-old Karrie informed her dad (very quickly), "Mom brought IMITATION pancakes, Daddy!"

Seven-year-old Jesse had come to the table straight from

the bathroom where he had been searching for something. His little sister, four-year-old Daisy, was seated at the table, and she asked, "Where have you been, Jesse?"

"In the bathroom, Daisy," Jesse said. "Why?"

"YOU were in the BATHROOM, Jesse, and I didn't hear any WATER running! Don't YOU touch any of MY food!"

It is the 1913-14 school year. Since their father worked for the railroad company that owned the railroad tracks close to where they lived, nine-year-old Bessie and her seven-year-old brother, Earl, felt comfortable walking alongside those tracks up the steep hill to the schoolhouse there at the top.

One particular engineer became a familiar sight to them, as his scheduled run was always while they were walking to school. One morning, as his engine passed them, the engineer released some steam, coal smoke, and soot, making the children dirty from head to foot! So they had to return home, get cleaned up again, and change their clothes before going on to school. Needless to say, they were very late.

The first time this happened, they thought it might have been an accident, but when it happened the second time, and ESPECIALLY when they saw the obvious delight on the face of the engineer, they KNEW it wasn't an accident!

Between the two of them, they decided how they would teach this dirty engineer a lesson. (And get even with him at the same time!) Before his next scheduled run, Bessie and Earl, armed with many bars of homemade laundry soap (popular at the time), set to work applying, by hand, soap to each one of the two rails of the railroad track on that steep hill (all the way to the top)!

The following morning, on schedule, they were walking along beside the tracks, going up the steep hill on their way to school, when, also on schedule, the train was coming. However, THIS time the engineer was having trouble keeping the engine's wheels turning on the slicked-up rails on the steep hill! Laughing happily, Bessie and Earl kept right on walking alongside the tracks, up the steep hill to the schoolhouse at the top, and the more the engine's wheels spun, the funnier they thought it was!

School had already taken up by the time the train reached the top of the hill, and in the quiet schoolroom all of the children listened to its slow progress as it fought its way over the top.

That engineer was furious! When he cornered Bessie and Earl's father at work later, his face was crimson as he told about what had happened. "I even used up all the sand from my sandbox gettin' to the top of that hill," he yelled, "and THEN I almost didn't make it! Not only that, the schedule was goofed up for the rest of the trip. Those BRATS should be HORSE-WHIPPED for greasin' up those tracks!" he screamed.

Their dad yelled right back, "IT served you RIGHT! I got a good look at them kids when they came home all black like that."

So, the issue was dropped, and Bessie and Earl continued to walk alongside the railroad tracks, up the steep hill, to the schoolhouse at the top. The engineer continued his scheduled runs, past them, up the steep hill, and beyond. Although, for SOME reason, the engineer didn't seem to see them after that!

While sitting with her mother, in the waiting room of the doctor's office, five-year-old Darcy watched as a young man with long hair came in and sat down. Little Darcy kept looking at the man for some time before going over to her mother and saying, "MOMMY! THAT daddy is a MOMMY!"

His older sister had been listening to five-year-old Terry excitedly telling about all of the small roadside apples he had seen. The two of them decided to take a sack and gather some the next day. As they walked along the road, Terry would bend down, pick one up, put it in the sack, then another, and another. His sister, later, was laughing and telling their father, "Those were NOT apples, Daddy. They were HORSE DROPPINGS!"

One very cold, snowy, and windy winter morning, five-year-

26

old Jennifer and her grandmother were sitting in front of the stove. Her grandmother was watching Jennifer dreamily stare off into space. After watching for a few minutes, in a soft tone of voice (so as not to break the spell), she asked, "What you are thinking about, Jennifer?"

Jennifer didn't change her expression when she asked, "Do you know how to can a bear, Grandma?"

Grandma said, "No, Jennifer. Do YOU know how to can a bear?"

She looked sort of surprised but answered quickly, "Why, SURE, Grandma! First, you go up on the mountain and kill a bear. Then you cut the bear up in little chunks and put these chunks in a can, put a lid on the can, and shake the can very, very hard."

When asked WHY she would shake the can so hard, she answered, "Why, Grandma, THAT'S to shake the SPIT out of the bear so you can EAT it!"

———————————

Taking the city bus across town, six-year-old Benjamin and his mother brought a supply of water to an elderly friend when his water pipes froze.

When they got to his house with the water, they found his house to be very cold, his refrigerator was empty, and he was dressed in several layers of old clothes. Although he was wearing slippers, he didn't have any socks on his feet. He hadn't shaved for a few days, either. In short, he looked pretty rough!

Little Benjamin stood there just looking at him for a few minutes, swallowed a couple of times, then said, "I'VE been saving MY money for the POOR! I've been saving it, but, Mommy took it and used it for the bus-fare!"

———————————

The family were all seated around the table at the Snake-Pit (a local café) for breakfast. The little girl, about six years of age, picked up the menu that was lying in front of her, looked at it for a few minutes, then, slamming it noisily onto the table, said, "I don't know why I'm looking at THIS! I can't read!"

Dave had been given permission to have Mike, a buddy of his, spend the night with him. And it was at GRANDMA'S, too! The two six-year-old boys decided to eat some applesauce. When the jar was brought out and set on the table, Mike asked, "HEY! What is THAT stuff?"

"Applesauce," he was told.

"Well, MY mom gets applesauce out of a can," Mike said.

"WELL, my GRANDMA gets applesauce out of an APPLE!" Dave told him.

"Aunt Patsy, where does the moon get its light from? Who turns it on and off?" little four-year-old Joshua asked.

To which his Aunt Patsy explained, "When Jehovah created our universe, He made the sun, moon, and Earth. And He made the moon to reflect light from the sun."

"Oh," Joshua replied. "Then the Earth has its own MIR-ROR!"

One day, four-year-old Dana's grandmother came to visit. She asked, "Where is Lars-Cat, Dana?"

In a disgusted tone of voice, Dana said, "Oh, he's out there GIRLIN' again, Grandma! But when we find him, we're gonna have his MEOWER taken out!"

Four days left until Christmas, and the family Christmas tree STILL hadn't been decorated! The subject was brought up for a family discussion, with: "We HAVE to fix the tree, now."

To which four-year-old Jesse asked, "Fix the tree? Oh, NO! I wonder who BROKE it?"

After taking her bath, the little three-year-old sweetheart asked her mother, "Would you cut my FOOT-NAILS, Mommy?"

It wasn't too long after his being toilet-trained that the toddler was out on a hunting trip with his daddy. He said, "I have to go tinkle, Daddy."

His daddy told him, "Go tinkle over there on a tree." And every time the toddler needed to go, he went on a tree.

At home one evening, the little guy went into the kitchen where everyone was sitting around the table and told his daddy that he had to go tinkle. His dad (not thinking) told him, "You know where to go." So, into the living room, and SURE ENOUGH, the boy "went tinkle" on the CHRISTMAS TREE!

One day, while a family was taking their garbage to the dump, some resident ravens were startled and (naturally) flew up into the air, causing the little two-year-old girl to cry out, "Mommy, Daddy! Look at the RAISINS!"

Up until recently, little eighteen-month-old Christopher hadn't had very much to do with his Uncle Roger. Then, one day while Christopher was at his uncle's house, Uncle Roger made a platter of eggs and toast. About six or eight slices of toast, enough for some toast for little Christopher, too. Since Christopher dearly LOVED toast, he was, naturally, watching from around the corner as his uncle sat down to eat. Well, when he gave Christopher some toast, too, all of a sudden Uncle Roger became a REAL GOOD GUY! And later, as the visitors were preparing to leave, they were saying good-bye when little Christopher went over, gave his uncle a great big hug and kiss, then said, "NOW! More TOAST, Uncie Roger!"

A young mother of three children had given her divorce

lawyer her promise that she would do her BEST to pay him within a year. And, by the end of that year, she had managed to save enough money to keep her word!

One day she stopped in at his office with the final payment and all three of her children with her. Leaving them seated in the outer office, she stepped into the lawyer's private office for a short consultation, after which she wanted him to meet her children.

Before stepping back into the outer office, she attempted a grandstand play. While proudly stating, "And THIS is the young fella we fought so hard to keep!" she swung open the office door, at the precise time that little two-year-old Daniel was busy letting the whole, wide world know that HE was VERY unhappy, with his gutsy cry of, "WAAAAH!"

Her lawyer looked at her for a moment, then, while smiling slightly, said, "So THAT'S what we worked so hard for!" and just shook his head.

During the time she was trying to introduce her two older girls, little Daniel kept on making a lot of noise AND tears, so she finally just gave up! Her lawyer just quietly walked off, all the time shaking his head.

While being potty-trained three-year-old Heather would get a cookie for being a GOOD GIRL every time she went potty. One day, while in the process of moving, the family stopped at a gas station and little Heather and her mother went into the public rest room there. While they were in one stall, someone else came in and went into an adjoining stall. Naturally, she could be heard going to the bathroom. So, little Heather bent down and looked into that stall, telling the lady there, "YOU are a GOOD GIRL!"

When three-and-a-half-year-old Matthew saw some reindeer on television, he said, "Hey! Look at those cows; they have STICKS on their heads!"

A grandpa and grandma were going to take everyone out to eat. Their 1971 Chrysler had an electric front seat leveler, as well as fold-down armrests (which the children just LOVED to sit on).

Little five-year-old Daniel was sitting on his "special seat" and was watching his grandma working the levers to get her side of the front seat to match his grandpa's side (so a third person could share their seat). Little Daniel was pretty impressed, as he said, "Grandma, you and Grandpa sure do have a COLD car! I'm gonna buy ME one just like it!"

Little Christi crawled into bed with her pregnant mother, and Mom decided to share a woman-to-woman chat with her. "Christi, the baby moved last night!"

Christi instantly responded, "Oh, no! Where did it go?"

Tony was a captain in the army. The following conversation was held with his five-year-old nephew, Paul.

"Uncle Tony?"

"Yes, Paul?"

"Something's been bothering me. There is something I want to know. . . . You're a captain, right?"

"Yes, Paul."

"Well, WHERE is your ship?"

"Milk comes from cows, right, Mom? Does orange juice come from horses?"

It seemed to everyone that eight-year-old Jordon was just always hungry. One day, when he said, "I'm hungry, Grandmother; could I have something to eat?" his grandmother asked, "Jordon, have you EVER been anything BUT hungry?"

Jordon quickly answered, "Once!"

31

Twelve-year-old Jennifer, being the oldest grandchild of the eight, decided to REALLY get into the Easter festivities at their grandparents' house. Using her own money, she bought special gifts for each of her five cousins who lived in a neighboring state.

As Easter drew closer and closer, Jennifer was getting more and more excited, and finally she divulged her secret to her grandmother when, calling from school one day, Jennifer asked, "Grandma, what is Aunt Sandy's phone number?"

To which her grandmother asked, "Why do you want your Aunt Sandy's phone number, Jennifer?"

Jennifer then explained (with great pride) what she had been doing and that she wanted to let her Aunt Sandy know what NOT to buy for all of the little ones!

Jennifer's grandmother praised her for her kind thoughtfulness and told her that she was a very sweet girl, adding, "It wouldn't be a good idea to call Aunt Sandy now, because of the long-distance charges, Jennifer."

Jennifer quickly replied, "Oh, it won't cost us anything, Grandma! I'll call her COLLECT!"

A young boy, about seven-and-one-half years old, was asked, "How do you like school?"

His face lit up, and with a great big smile he instantly replied, "OH! I LOVE it. They're TEACHING me something!"

Little three-and-a-half-year-old Unti was playing hide-and-go-seek with a cousin of his. Since he had never played the game before, it took him a little time before he knew just what to do. It was Unti's turn to "go seek," he had his eyes closed, and he overheard his cousin say, "I just don't know WHERE to hide. . . ."

Unti said, "Hide in the closet and I'll pretend that I don't know where you are!"

Later, when he was hiding, he chose to hide under the desk and called out, "Ready or not . . . here I am!"

The cat was sleeping on its back, with its legs all stretched out, and when little three-year-old Crystal saw this, she excitedly called out, "Grandma! Look, Kitty is sleeping wrong side out!"

While their mother was talking to their grandmother on the telephone, four-year-old Jake and two-and-a-half-year-old Barney decided to go bowling (using fresh eggs!) on the couch! After hanging up the telephone and noticing how quiet everything was in the living room, their mother went in to check. She found that the boys had gone through ONE DOZEN eggs in their bowling game!

Daisy's pregnant mother had taken three-and-a-half-year-old Daisy with her on one of her regular visits to the doctor. When the doctor talked about the PUPPIES in her mommy's tummy, little Daisy quickly let him know, "Those AREN'T puppies! That's Baby WHOZIT!"

The young family was preparing to board the train bound for Colorado. Little four-year-old Patsy was (tearfully) telling her beloved grandmother good-bye.

Her grandmother, while telling Patsy good-bye and trying to make things just a little easier, told Patsy, "Be sure to help your mother with little Irvin and Billie, now."

"Yes, Grandma, I know," Patsy said. "We don't want Momma to have a NERVOUS WRECK!"

Mom and Dad had just returned home and stepped into the kitchen, where the three young brothers, Mike, Bob, and John, were very busy with a mixing bowl, a gallon of milk, and two pounds of butter. One of the boys was cutting the butter into a crock, another one was adding milk, and the third boy was stirring.

Their mother asked, "WHAT ON EARTH are you boys DOING?"

To which they proudly answered, "WE are making BUTTER-MILK!"

A Harrison, Idaho, area site was chosen for a summer campground by a group of churches (of different religions). Going together, they hired a pleasant elderly gentleman, with snow-white hair, to maintain the campgrounds for the summer.

His little four-year-old granddaughter asked, "Grandpa, were you on Noah's ark?"

When he answered, "No," she asked "How did you keep from drowning, Grandpa?"

Two first-grade students were walking down the hall. They passed Mr. Kopel, who was walking up the hall, and greeted him with, "Good morning, Mr. Kopel."

Mr. Kopel said, "Good morning."

Mr. Horvath, who resembled Mr. Kopel, was closely follow-ing Mr. Kopel up the hallway. The two first-graders greeted Mr. Horvath with, "Good morning, Mr. Kopel."

Mr. Horvath said, "Good morning," and kept walking up the hallway.

One of the students turned and said to the other, "Hey . . . didn't we say good morning to him TWICE?"

The students at the state school for the deaf were instructed, "ANYTHING important that happens to you, you write and tell your folks."

One day the parents of this seven-year-old boy received the following letter:

Dear Momma and Dad:

A mouse ran across the floor!

Love,
Finley

It was a few years ago when this story took place. The names have been changed to protect those involved.

Mr. Smith was a first-grade teacher in a small grade school. One morning, one of Mr. Smith's students very excitedly said, "Mr. Smith! Mr. Smith! My daddy shot a deer yesterday!"

Since it had been shot out of season, warnings of, "SSSHHH! Be QUIET! SSHH!" instantly came from her older brother and sister.

Quickly, and very emphatically, she let them know, "Oh, it's okay to tell HIM, 'cause THIS is Mr. SMITH!"

The young mother had started to give her two-year-old daughter a paddling when the little angel told her mother, "IF YOU want to spank MY panties, you take them OFF, first!"

Doris had always tried to protect the spiders at their house, trying to keep them from being killed. One day, her daughter Sherree (needing a spider for her biology class) talked Doris into letting her catch a spider to take to school.

Sherree washed a large jar, put some air holes in its lid, then put some leaves and grass into the jar and proceeded to locate and capture one of the spiders.

Now, Sherree was very proud of herself (and her spider!) and carried the jar around, showing off her spider. BUT, you guessed it, Sherree goofed! One time when she took the lid off the jar, her spider got away! Down onto the floor it went and crawled away as fast as it could.

Sherree, her older sister, Sandy, their mother, Doris, and even Sandy's two-year-old son, Terry, were instantly looking for the spider. Finally, Doris saw it and told little Terry, "There it is, Terry! Right there by your foot! Get it, hon!"

Which Terry did. As he stomped it with his little foot, he was proudly saying, "I DID, Grandma! I got 'im! I got 'im!"

A person might be surprised at the tender age at which young children can start picking up vibes from their elders. For example, when her daddy comes in from work (sort of grumpy), little two-year-old Emily gives him a quick kiss and hug, then, while leaning back and looking at him, asks, "Daddy tired?"

It was four-year-old Jesse's day to go shopping with his mother for Christmas presents for his family and friends. In the stores, there was lots of candy on display, causing little Jesse to say, "Candy, candy, candy! Candy, candy, candy! Don't they know that Christmas means toys . . . and Jesus?"

This little boy, about four years old, had gone with his family to see the movie *Twenty Thousand Leagues under the Sea*, which, as everyone knows, is a VERY scary movie (especially for young kids).

After watching the part where the tentacles of the giant octopus appeared to come through the portholes at the edge of the screen, the little guy needed to go to the rest room. But when he and his daddy got there, LO AND BEHOLD!, there were those small round toilets for them to use! It was obvious that he was pretty scared when he backed away from them.

Grinning slightly, his dad asked, "What's the matter, Son?"

With a shaky voice, he answered that with a question: "There won't be a AUTO-ON-A-PUSS come out of THERE, will there, Daddy?"

Little Daniel had just celebrated his fifth birthday on a Friday. Then, while spending the weekend at his grandparents' home, he called his daddy (long-distance) for a nice visit via telephone. On Sunday, they took him back home.

On Sunday evening, while Daniel was in the process of getting acquainted with his mother's new boyfriend, Michael, everyone was sitting in the kitchen around the table, drinking coffee and visiting. Daniel's grandpa asked, "How old were you when your dad died, Michael?"

Michael answered, "I was seven years old."

"That's a coincidence," Grandpa said. "I was seven years old when MY dad died!"

Little Daniel was sitting on Grandma's lap. He looked down at his hands and, in a very quiet, low voice, said, "I was seven years old when MY daddy died, too!"

The topic of conversation among the fifth-grade students was the age of their new substitute teacher. Then, the question was put to the teacher.

The teacher said, "Well, we'll put it this way: my youngest child is a thirteen-year old girl."

To which one boy replied, "I have a brother that is fourteen years old and my mother is forty, so you are real close to my mother's age . . . right?"

Smiling, the teacher said, "That suits me just fine."

Another girl, very quietly, stated, "Ahh . . . she has to be AT LEAST SIXTY!"

On that very important day, of registering Benjamin for kindergarten, Ben's sister, three-and-a-half-year old Daisy, and their little brother, two-year-old Rick, were invited into the classroom to meet Benjamin's teacher and some of his class-mates and to play with the kindergarten toys . . . in general, just to look around. So, little Rick played with the building blocks and Daisy put some of one of the puzzles in place. After their mother had finished with the registration procedure and had visited with the kindergarten teacher for a short time, they all went to McDonald's for lunch!

All of the above took place shortly before the first day of school.

The first day of school, Benjamin's daddy gave Benjamin a ride to school on his way to work. After school, Benjamin's mother, with little Daisy and little Rick, walked over to school to walk Benjamin home.

While walking along toward the school, little Daisy asked, "Mommy, are we going to pick Benjamin up?"

Her mother said, "That's right, Daisy." She could see that Daisy was thinking (because she had her "thinking face" on) and was expecting Daisy to say something about the fun she had had there in Benjamin's classroom. However, she was wrong.

Instead, little Daisy asked, "Mommy, why do we HAVE to pick Benjamin up? Why can't we just LEAVE him there?"

One father had taken pictures of the hospital, the delivery room, the equipment used, the different technicians, the nurses, and the doctors involved in the delivery of the new baby. Yes, he took home quite a stack of pictures to show the two older boys when he brought their mother and the new baby home from the hospital. In going through the pictures, he pointed out the doctor who had delivered the baby and the nurses who had helped the doctor deliver the baby, as well as the nurse(s) who took care of the new baby (bathed, fed, changed diapers, etc., etc.). Little three-year-old Brett looked squarely at his mother and asked, "And what were YOU doing all this time?"

The frustrated young mother was obviously upset when her four-year-old son wanted her to buy EVERYTHING that HE saw on the shelves in the store. Finally, she knelt down in front of him and, face to face, told him in a VERY firm voice, "Now, YOU watch my mouth; YOU read my lips. When I say N-O, I MEAN NO!"

To which the little boy quickly replied, "But, Mom, we BOTH know that I don't know how to read!"

Little four-year-old Bryan was anxiously waiting for his turn at confessions. When his turn came, he excitedly jumped up, turned around, and asked, "What do I do now?"

While recuperating from surgery, the little boy had been confined to his bed. One day, while playing with the telephone, he complained to his mother, "I ALWAYS get the HOSPITAL!"

"What do you mean?" his mother asked.

He answered, "They ALWAYS tell me, 'OPERATION! OPERA-TION!' "

Little Frankie was on his first hunting trip with his dad and mother. The small hunting party came to a place in the road where a bear had relieved himself. Frankie told his mother and dad, "Wasn't that nice of that old bear? . . . He stacked some BERRIES for us!"

When four-year-old Daniel wet his pants, Michael told him, "Now, THAT'S enough of THIS!"

Daniel quickly responded with, "Let's talk about THAT when I get OLDER!"

On a trip to the coast, while passing the U & I Sugar Company, three-year-old Butch's grandmother said, "Look there, Butch. That's where they make U & I sugar." A small discussion took place and soon dropped.

On the return trip, by the U & I Sugar Company, little Butch excitedly shook his grandmother's arm, saying, "Look, Grandma! THAT'S where you and ME'S made!"

Little three-and-a-half-year old Linda had a favorite neighborhood friend, and she would slip off (unnoticed) and go three or four doors down the street to this neighbor's house to visit, have cookies and milk with them, and stay until her by then frantic mother came to take her back home.

One day, Linda's parents decided to talk to her, telling her, "Linda, you just HAVE to stop doing this, because you never tell us where you are going and a lot of time AND energy is spent in looking for you. It ALWAYS scares us, because we don't know where you are . . . maybe you are lost(?) or maybe you are hurt!"

So little Linda promised that she wouldn't do that anymore. She kept her promise for about three or four months. Then, one day, Linda was missing, again! Her poor mother looked EVERYWHERE for her and, not finding her, called Linda's father, and he came home to look for Linda, too. The frantic parents were about to call the police to help them search for Linda when the mother thought to call Linda's neighborhood friend, and SURE ENOUGH, Linda was there having a cookie and watching television with them!

Linda's dad went down to get Linda, promising her a spanking when they got home. After the spanking, he asked, "Now, Linda, do YOU know WHY I gave you that spanking?"

Linda answered "Yes." Then, nose to nose with her daddy, she said, "Because YOU hate MY guts!"

Her three-year-old grandson was watching his new baby sister nursing at her mother's breast. He told his grandmother, "Those usta was mine, Grandma!"

Little six-year-old Jeramy had gone to the Washington State Fair with his grandpa and grandma. While they were there, balloons on sticks had been purchased for the kids. Later, on their way home, little Jeramy asked his Grandpa to take his balloon off the stick for him.

40

After Grandpa had tried and tried, finally giving up, he told little Jeramy, "I'm sorry, Casey [nickname]; I just can't get that balloon off that stick."

To which Jeramy replied, "That's OK, Grandpa. After all, you're an old man!"

———————

Little Kandi was very happy and proud to go to kindergarten. She went to school every day . . . no problem. However, when it came time for her to go to school the following year . . . NO WAY! When her grandmother asked her just WHY she didn't want to go to school, Kandi replied, "I CAN'T go to school, Grandma, 'cause I don't know how to read and write!"

———————

Little Josh was proud telling his grandfather, "I got myself my first window, Grandpa!"

His grandfather was instantly on edge. With raised eyebrows (and raised voice), he asked, "YOU did WHAT?"

"I did, Grandpa; I got myself a window!" he said. "Mommy and Daddy don't know about it, yet."

———————

The middle-aged man and his wife (who has premature white hair) were out for an evening stroll in a small town. As they were passing a house where some small children were playing up in the porch, one of the little boys called out, "Hello, old woman! Hello, old woman!"

Not answering, she just looked up at her husband as he smiled down at her. Then the little boy called out, "Hello, old man!"

———————

It was a community project. A group of people was working at cleaning the Nine-Mile Cemetery grounds, cutting brush, pulling weeds, and raking and burning leaves. Everyone was working hard to get the cemetery grounds cleaned up, after having gone through another long, hard winter.

Little five-and-a-half-year-old Billy while helping his aunt (who was one of the workers) asked her, "Well, why do we need to clean all THIS up if they are ALL dead?"

Frank's family was new in the neighborhood. One warm spring day, he decided to change the tires around on their car when a pretty little (approximately five-year-old) neighborhood girl stopped by to watch. A conversation soon developed, and Frank asked her, "What does your mommy do?"

"My mommy is a nurse," she told him.

"Oh, that's nice," Frank said. "I'll bet when YOU grow up, you'll want to be a nurse, just like your mommy?"

To which she answered very quickly, "Oh, NO! When I grow up I'M going to go on WELFARE, so I can do anything I want!"

After getting a spanking at school from the teacher, little Calvin came running in from kindergarten (which was right next door), telling his mother, "I hate Mrs. Swan! She's SO mean and onery! I don't like her at all! I HATE her!"

It so happened at this time Mrs. Swan stopped in to see Calvin's mother about a completely different matter. (In fact, the spanking wasn't even mentioned!) Calvin met her at the door. He was talking away about a mile a minute about this, that, and the other, "BLAH! BLAH! BLAH!" Then, just as SOON as Mrs. Swan left, little Calvin started in on her, again: "I HATE Mrs. Swan! I HATE her," etc., etc.

On Sunday afternoon in Barney's (a local supermarket), I was doing my weekly grocery shopping and my shopping cart was VERY full. While the cashier was ringing up my grocery bill, I thought of something else I needed and went back to get it.

While I was gone, a man (with his three-year-old daughter riding in his cart) got into line directly behind my cart. As I walked past them back to my cart, his daughter, Michelle, turned and offered me a one-dollar bill!

Her daddy looked down at Michelle and, while smiling, said, "Michelle figured that with a cart as full as yours, you needed ALL the help you could get!"

Daniel's grandmother likes to make up poems. One day, she wanted to read one of her new poems to three-and-a-half-year-old Daniel.

After seeing all of the crossed-out markings (corrections) on her work sheet, little Daniel decided that he wouldn't listen, "Because, that's GARBAGE, Grandma!"

There's no doubt about it, television advertising gets its message across, as the following story will verify:

Keeping in mind the little song advertising Alka-Seltzer, "Plop, plop. Fizz, fizz. Get the FEEL-BETTER feeling that Alka-Seltzer gives!"

One day, a little three-year-old girl I'll call Beth was in the bathroom, excitedly calling for her daddy to, "Come QUICK, Daddy!"

Her daddy went in to find little Beth sitting on the toilet having a bowel movement! Beth told her daddy, "Listen Daddy! Plop! Plop! Fizz, fizz! BOY! What a BETTER feeling THAT is!"

Please keep in mind to a Baptist, getting baptized means getting WET. However, one young Baptist boy, approximately ten years of age, absolutely INSISTED that he would NOT get baptized! Although everything pointed to the fact that he WAS spiritually ready, he still said an emphatic, "NO!"

No one could understand why he didn't want to get batpized, so one day the minister had a talk with the boy, trying to find out just WHY he didn't want to get baptized. The boy gave the surprising answer: " 'Cause I don't want to get hit in the head!"

The minister then explained, "Ours is a small church, in a

43

small community. Our baptism pool has been home-made, constructed of metal with welded seams and with cement blocks underneath for extra support. During a baptism, as I put the person underwater, the movement of our weights combined with the movement of the water is what makes the metal pool clank and bang! I don't hit ANYONE in the head!"

Twelve-year-old Jennifer was bragging to her grandfather one day. "Grandpa," she said, "I can set MY body-clock and get up at ANY time I want to!"

"And, just HOW do you do THAT, Jennifer?" Grandpa asked.

"Why, I do it by the amount of water I drink before I go to bed!" was her smug reply.

Now, these parents had tried very hard to instill the wise teachings of BOTH books of the Bible in their children, right from the start. One day, when their ten-year-old son got into serious trouble at school, his parents asked him, "And just what do YOU think we should do to you about this?"

He thought for a short time, then answered, "STONE me!"

Jimmy and his friend Steve were in the same kindergarten class and, since they were also neighbors, walked to and from school together.

One day, Jimmy and Steve were on their way home from school and Jimmy spotted a rock out in the road. The rock had such a sparkle that Jimmy went into the road and picked it up. Steve saw how pretty and shiny the rock was, and since it sparkled so brightly, the boys decided it was GOLD!

Steve wanted the rock, but remember, Jimmy saw it first, so they got into a fight.

When Jimmy came in for lunch SO dirty, his mother asked, "What on EARTH happened to YOU?"

Then, Jimmy told her about his finding this gold nugget out

in the street and how Steve wanted to steal it from him and about the fight they had gotten into!

Jimmy's mother asked, "Who won?"

"I don't know," Jimmy said, "but I found out that I can run FASTER than Steve!"

Five-year-old Daniel, while stretching both arms straight out, told his grandfather, "I love you THIS much, Grandpa!"

His grandfather asked, "Is THAT all, Daniel?"

Little Daniel, obviously taking a second thought, said, "I can't reach any FARTHER, Grandpa!"

The little five-year-old boy was sitting next to an older lady in church one Sunday morning. When the offering plate was passed, he looked up at the lady and, in a very serious manner, asked her, "Do we pay God now?"

Two-year-old Terry's mother, Sandy, had worked at the Montgomery Ward's store and knew the different salespeople there.

One day, not too long before her second baby was born, Sandy took Terry into the Montgomery Ward's shoe department to buy him his first pair of cowboy boots.

Now, knowing Sandy, the Negro shoe salesman asked Terry, "I understand that you'll be having a new little baby around your house. Are you excited about that?"

To which little Terry quickly answered, "YOU BET! And it's gonna be BLACK, too!"

Before you read these next two stories, please keep in mind, in this area of our great country, for some reason, there are few Negroes. Many of the small children that are raised here seldom

45

(if ever) have SEEN them! Hence, the first time they do can be quite an experience for all concerned.

Two-year-old Johnny was at a school basketball game with his dad. Johnny started getting fussy, so his dad took him out into the hall for a drink of water. While they were standing there in the hallway, Johnny's dad saw a Negro girl holding her infant baby, so they went over to see her baby. Johnny's daddy said, "See the little baby, Johnny. Isn't he cute?"

To which little Johnny quickly replied, "Daddy . . . THAT baby has a BROWN head!"

Barbara was in the Two Swabbies in Spokane at closing time when her eighteen-month-old son, Johnny, noticed a black man behind them. As they were going through the checkout counter, Barbara held her breath, hoping that Johnny wouldn't say anything, since he'd never seen a black person before. But just as the cashier handed them their receipt and they started out the door, Johnny blurted out, "Brown head, the brown head!"

Six-year-old Brian is one of five children and is a friendly, outgoing, and lovable first-grader. It is evident that his baby sister, one-year-old Katie, is number one in his heart, as he is ALWAYS talking about his cute baby sister, how pretty she is, and the cute things she does.

At open house, Brian was thrilled to have the privilege of introducing little Katie. He took Katie by the hand, and together they walked to the front of the schoolroom. Then, in a VERY clear voice, Brian said, "Everyone that thinks Katie is pretty, please raise your hand!"

The following story took place at the time Frankie Lane's song "I Want To Go Where the Wild Goose Goes" was so popular.

One morning, six-year-old Molly ran into her mother's bedroom, waking her up. Molly said, "Mommy, wake up and go fix my breakfast!"

This was VERY unusual conduct for Molly, so her mother asked, "WHY? What's going on?"

Molly told her, "I wanna go where the WILD GOOSE has gone!"

———————————

This little six-year-old boy was simply a GOOD student. He was neat, well mannered, and punctual about turning in his homework, which was always correct and neat, as well as always bringing back his books to his teacher.

His first day back at school after having had chicken pox, he got to school without his book! He had this to say to his teacher: "I had too many things to remember crammed in my head and there just wasn't room for one more! YOU know what THAT'S like, don't you, Mrs. Austin?"

———————————

It was seven-year-old Ben's first cavity. When his daddy took him to the dentist, who was an old friend, they were visiting with each other instead of explaining to Ben what he should expect from his tooth, and NO ONE explained it before the dentist deadened and filled the tooth.

Later that evening, while at supper, Ben left the table without eating and went to his room. His mother found him lying on his bed crying. "I wish I had just let my tooth hurt like it did before!" he sobbed. "At LEAST, I COULD eat, and my bottom lip won't be stuck straight out for the rest of my life."

———————————

Barbara was talking to her children about the family reunion and telling them everyone in the family who would be coming. (Of course, they wanted her to name EVERYONE.) She had started naming the aunts: "Aunt Vickie, Aunt Pam, Aunt Joanne,

Aunt Valerie, Aunt Kristen" when her seven-year-old son, Travis, said, "Antarctica!"

While giving her seven-year-old grandson a ride to the ballpark, Eileen realized (too late) that he had left his sunglasses at home. Being concerned that the sun was too bright for his eyes, she kindly offered him the use of his grandfather's cap, which was lying on the seat between them.

Which he VERY emphatically declined: "OH NO! I'm not BALD, Grandma!"

Because of his speech impediment, little three-and-a-half-year-old Ricky went to a special speech therapy class. He was transported, to and from his class, via a small school bus, driven by a lady (a friend of his mother).

One day, the doctor visited the class to check the progress of the children. Little Ricky was apparently influenced by the doctor's personality, as later he told his mother, "I am going to be a doctor, when I grow up!"

His mother wanted little Ricky's daddy to hear him say it. But when she asked, Ricky, "Tell Daddy what you are going to be when you grow up?" Ricky told his daddy, "I'm going to be a doctor AND a daddy, when I grow up!"

Later, Ricky's mother wanted him to tell her friend (Ricky's school-bus driver) what he was going to be when he grew up. He said, "I'm going to be a doctor and a daddy AND a MOMMY, when I grow up!"

Three-year-old Crystal would stay in her bedroom playing with her toys all day without complaining. At night, however, she would NOT go to her room! One day, her grandmother asked her, "WHY don't you like your room at night, Crystal? It's the same room that you play in all day long."

Little Crystal answered, "I can't go in there at night, Grandma, 'cause I can't open my EYES!"

48

At the family dinner table one evening, while eating supper with his family, the little three-and-a-half-year-old boy suddenly burst into tears, and for no apparent reason! After a few moments of many tears and much sobbing, he told his mother and father, "While I was chewing my food, my teeth stepped on my tongue!"

It was the first day of kindergarten, and since Hakon was scheduled for the afternoon class, his mother decided to take him out to lunch before his class started. As their lunch progressed (and schooltime approached), Hakon developed a stomachache. He said, "My stomach hurts, Mom. Do I HAVE to go to school?"

Trying to reassure him, his mother told him, "Once you get started, you'll find that your stomachache will go away, and everything will be OK. You'll see."

However, Hakon STILL insisted that he didn't want to go to school because of his stomachache.

Then his mother told him, "I had a stomachache on MY first day of school also, but IT went away. And YOUR stomachache will go away; you'll see."

To which Hakon replied, "Well . . . will a HEADACHE do?"

It had been the accepted practice to allow lurid pictures from *Playboy* magazine to be displayed on the bedroom walls of the on-call firemen at the Wallace, Idaho, fire hall, and when the kindergarten children came on the annual visit to the fire hall all of the doors to rooms bearing such pictures were securely closed (and checked).

However . . . On one such visit to the fire hall, all such loose material had been removed and doors had been closed, etc., the students had been shown through the fire hall, questions had been answered, and things had gone smoothly. The children were then given a snorkle-ride, which was in the basket and lifted them two or three stories high.

On the first ride, the two young boys came down, giggling and whispering to the others, who would in turn giggle as well! The fire chief thought, *Hey! What's going on here? They shouldn't be acting like that!*

It was soon discovered that the curtains at the window of one of the bedrooms with the pictures had been left open, thus allowing full vision through that window, of the *Playboy* pictures on the wall of that room to the children up there in the basket!

———————

In the process of the "I CAN—GOD CAN" children's sermon two cans had been placed in the front of the room. One can carried the label: "I can" and the other can carried the label: "God can." Different subjects would be brought up and discussed; then the children would decide which can each subject belonged in. Should it be "I can" or should it be "God can"?

The subject getting along with brothers and sisters was brought up, and a little six-year-old girl said, "THAT definitely has to be the GOD can!"

———————

Two-year-old Robby was being introduced to the Nativity scene. He asked, "Who are THOSE people?"

He was told, "That is Mary, and that is Baby Jesus, and that is God. Now, Robby, YOU tell ME who they are."

So . . . Robby said, "That is Mary Elizabeth, and that is Jesus."

When asked, "Who is that other guy?" Robby thought for a minute, then said, "OH! THAT IS BOB!"

———————

Good deeds done at home was the topic being discussed by the primary Sunday school class.

A little boy stood up and (obviously very proud) stated, "I do a good deed at home, and I do it EVERY Sunday morning!"

He was questioned about WHAT good deed it was that he did.

And (smiling from ear to ear) he stuck out his chest and proudly said, "I help Mommy and Daddy carry out the BEER bottles EVERY Sunday morning!"

"Scott, put this change in the offering plate."

"Is it for God and Jesus? Don't they have any money?"

While coming out of the grocery store, I saw a little girl (about six years old) and her younger brother (about four years old), with their small dog. The little girl was holding the dog's leash, which she wanted her brother to hold while she went into the store first. But he told her that HE wanted to go first . . . and he did.

I stopped for a moment to tell her, "That sure is a cute little dog you have."

Proudly she told me, "Thank you."

At that time, my husband called to me, "Now, Mary, don't you get into a DOG-FIGHT!" (A family joke.)

The little girl took him serious, though, telling me, "Oh, HE won't fight! He's friendly. He likes EVERYONE!"

So, I bent down to pet her dog and scratch behind his ears, while asking, "What is his name?"

"Coco," she said.

Then I asked, "How old is Coco?"

"He is two years old," she answered, adding, "Really, he's an OLD MAN, but at our house he's only two!"

Before going to sleep one night, six-year-old Darrell was lying in his bed, crying. His mother went in to see what his problem was, and he said, "I feel odd. I don't have any friends."

His mother said, "Oh yes, you have; you have LOTS of friends." Then she named three of them.

"That's not enough," he told her.

His mother said, "I'll be your friend, too."

To which Darrell replied, "THAT won't help. . . . Then, I'll feel odd again!"

Since the family car didn't have air-conditioning, the fan used for circulation of air was used for cooling. One hot summer day, six-year-old Cheree asked, "Mommy, would you turn on the cold heat?"

While saying good night to his cousins, four-year-old Benjamin decided that he liked their compact car. He asked, "Where did you get this car?"

"I bought it. What do you want to know for?" was the answer.

"Oh, I like it REAL good," Benjamin said, "and I want Daddy to buy me one JUST like it!"

While her family was taking some garbage to the dump in their old pickup truck, little four-year-old Daisy was obviously upset. She wanted to know, "Daddy, will you stop this pickup and tell your spiders to get out?"

Four-year-old Allen was sitting in the kitchen watching his mother fix lunch for Charles, his baby brother. She was chopping up his food for him.

Later, when she asked Allen if he wanted some squash for his lunch, he said, "NO THANK YOU! I wouldn't care for MINE to be all squashed!"

Christi was seated on an airplane. "When do we get to fly upside down?" she asked.

The little boy was SO thrilled when their friends stopped in to visit a few days after Thanksgiving. He met them at the door and very excitedly pulled Alice into the kitchen, opened the freezer door, proudly showing her their freezer full of deer meat (shot out of season?), with the proud explanation: "Look at ALL that TURKEY we have!"

Dorothy's eight-year-old grandson was selling Santa Claus candy, and he wanted his grandmother to buy herself a box of it from him. Dorothy had a weight problem (and candy IS fattening!), so when he asked her to buy a box of candy from him, she said, "I WOULD buy a box . . . but ONLY if you guarantee me that there will be NO calories in it."

He quickly assured her, "There won't be ANY calories in it."

Since he seemed so sure of himself, she couldn't help but ask, "How can you be so SURE there won't be calories in it?"

"You just buy the box, Grandma," he said. "I will PERSONALLY remove the candy and you won't have to worry about those old calories!"

Down through the years people have made many prophecies of the world coming to an end. One such a prophecy had been made naming the date and time. The following morning, Diana's mother got up, looked all around, then made the remark to seven-year-old Diana; "Well, I guess the world DIDN'T come to the end. . . . I'M still here!"

To which Diana answered, "How do you KNOW it didn't? Did you look outside yet?"

One day, Robby's neighbor told him, "Robby, our cat has had baby kittens and your cat, Mittens, is their father! They look JUST like him! I think you should take one of the kittens."

Later, when Robby told his mother about it, she said, "No, Robby, you cannot have one of the kittens. I don't think that

Mittens is their father, either. Why . . . they don't even LOOK like Mittens!"

Eight-year-old Robby (evidently wanting one of the kittens) argued, "But, Mom, I don't look like DAD!"

Little four-year-old Tim lives in a small town in upstate New York. The town is surrounded by farm and dairy country. Sometimes the area residents make a quick trip into town for something without taking the extra time to clean up first.

Now, Tim's parents own and operate a furniture store in town, and sometimes they are busy when someone comes into the store, so little Tim visits with the person until his folks get there. As you can imagine, he spends a lot of time at the store and tries to be helpful.

One day, one of the dairymen came into the store (evidently right out of the barn) to buy something from Tim's parents. Just a short time later, Tim comes into the store, holds his head back, and while making loud sniffing sounds says, "Hey! There's a COW in here! Someone left their COW here! Where's the cow?"

The family was gathered for Thanksgiving dinner, and a number of aunts, uncles, and cousins joined them around the food-laden table.

After grace was given, everyone started filling their plates while visiting with everyone else. Little four-and-a-half-year-old Bessie wanted a slice of bread. She asked, "May I have a slice of bread, please?"

No one heard her, so she waited a little while, then asked again, "May I PLEASE have a slice of bread?"

With all of the noise of the silverware on the dishes, of people eating and drinking, as well as of everyone STILL talking, she STILL wasn't heard. So . . . she asked a third time, "May I have a slice of bread?"

She waited for a VERY short time, then in an EXTRA loud voice yelled, "BR-R-READ . . . BREAD! BREAD! BREAD! BREAD!"

One morning, little Scott didn't want to wear his underwear. His pants were enough, and as he held his pants up, he said, "See, Mom? There are no holes!"

Mike and Jeanie, young parents-to-be, had gone to visit some friends who had a little three-year-old son. Little Jeff was in a phase where he liked to run and jump into a person, give her a hug, get down, and do it again!

When Jeff ran up to Jeanie, sitting on the couch, and jumped right into her lap, Mike took Jeff aside and explained to him, "Jeff, you shouldn't do that, because Jeanie has a baby in her tummy, and when you jump into her like you did, you might hurt the baby!"

A little later, Jeff made a run at Mike, piling into him, hugged him, got down, and made a run toward Jeanie . . . stopped, then thoughtfully turned and asked his mother, "If Aunt Jeanie has a baby in her tummy . . . how did it get there, Mommy? Did she EAT it?"

A logger was up in the woods one day with his wife and their three-and-a-half-year-old daughter. While her daddy was working, the little girl needed to go potty, so her mother had her sit on one of the logs in the deck. When her dad came up out of the timber where he had been working, she very excitedly told him, "Daddy! Daddy! I pottied over a LOG!"

Four-year-old Matthew was riding with his grandparents one day. A big semitruck loaded with chickens passed them. Since the load of chickens was such an enormous load, the remark was made: "Look at all of those chickens going to market."

Matthew's grandmother said, "I wonder if they know what is going to happen when they get where they are going?"

Little Matthew quickly replied, "Don't worry, Grandma; they don't even know where they're going when they don't have their head!"

After retiring from teaching school for thirty-five years, Mrs. Johnson offered her services as a substitute teacher in the school district.

One day, in a small elementary school, this little first-grade boy told her, "Chris told me that YOU don't know NOTHIN'!"

Jesse's mother had decided to keep his older sister, Ellie, home from school because she had laryngitis. Six-year-old Jesse wanted to know what THAT meant and was told that Ellie had lost her voice.

When Jesse went to school that morning, he told his first-grade teacher and class, "Ellie stayed home from school today because she LOST her VOICE!"

The following day, Ellie was able to go to school. Upon seeing her there, one of Jesse's classmates came up to her in the hallway and asked, "Where did you find your voice, Ellie?"

One little girl told her substitute teacher, "You are the dumbest teacher I've ever seen! You don't do ANYTHING the way MY teacher does!"

Six-year-old Ben came home from school with the reason WHY you shouldn't pet stray animals. "Mommy," he said, "you shouldn't pet stray puppies, because they might get foamy at the mouth and BITE you! And you might get BABIES!"

On a trip through Wyoming, six-year-old Cheree spotted

some antelope and (very excited) said, "HEY! Mom, Dad, look at the CANTALOUPE!"

———————————

Four-year-old Mike was upset with his grandfather for smoking, and he was trying ANYTHING and EVERYTHING to get his grandfather to stop.

One day, after someone had crashed into little Mike's grandfather's picket fence, a policeman was there (making a report of the accident), so little Mike went up to the officer and said, "Hello."

The officer, in turn, said, "Hello."

Mike said, "My name is Mike; what's YOUR name?"

And the officer told Mike that his name was Joe.

Then Mike asked, "Joe, would you please arrest my grandpa and put him in jail?"

"Well . . . WHY should I do THAT, Mike?" Joe asked.

To which Mike quickly answered, " 'Cause he won't quit SMOKING!"

———————————

Because of the mice in their house, four-year-old Matthew would NOT go into the kitchen alone! Not even in broad daylight! So, he would take his baby brother (in the stroller) along to protect him whenever he needed to go into the kitchen!

———————————

And another little four-year-old boy told his mother that HE wanted to be an inventor when he grew up.

"What would you like to invent?" his mother asked.

"UNDERPANTS!" was his quick answer.

His answer really surprised his mother, so she asked him, "Why underpants?"

He said, "Because . . . mine take too long to put on!"

———————————

Four-year-old Barbara was having a TERRIBLE time eating

her ice cream cone, which had a chocolate topping. It was a warm summer day, and melting ice cream and chocolate were all over her face and hands and arms. She asked, "Grandma, does ice cream MELT?"

Five-year-old Mike was listening to his grandmother telling him, "Eat plenty of fresh fruits and vegetables, and be sure to eat them RAW, because they are better for you raw."

To which Mike agreed, saying, "Yeah . . . like RAW MEAT!"

When kindergarten FINALLY started, little Jesse didn't think the school day was long enough. Everything was easy and LOTS of fun. He was having a good time and not getting very excited about any of his schoolwork. In other words, he was slow at completing his assignments.

One day, his teacher had a talk with him. "Now, Jesse," she said, "you are going to HAVE to get busy and get your work finished and turned in to me on time!"

Jesse replied asking, "Aw . . . what's the rush?"

Being a bird lover himself, Sid was always teaching his children about birds at every opportunity. One day, a cedar waxwing flew into their backyard, and Sid told the children all about that bird.

It was some time later, while riding down through Burke Canyon with his dad, that little five-year-old Fred spotted one of the cedar waxwing birds and said, "HEY! There's one of those GREASY FEATHER birds!"

Five-year-old Nancy had watched the advertising on television: "You take the key off of this product to this address in Spokane to see if YOU have won a new Chevrolet car!"

When her mother's car had mechanical problems and

Nancy's father had been working on it for a while, little Nancy couldn't help but advise, "Daddy, take the key over and see if you have won Mommy a NEW car!"

When Scott was three years old he was developmentally delayed, requiring help that involved a special school with "speech stimulation." One of their tactics was not giving a child anything unless he made an honest attempt to ask for it. Kathy, whom Scott loved dearly, was the head of this school.

When Scott turned six, Kathy came to his birthday party in his classroom. Scott was handing out the cupcakes. He handed one to Kathy, who graciously started to thank him. With a teasing grin, Scott started to take it back until Kathy asked him for the cupcake!

One day, little six-year-old Gail didn't want to eat all of her food. Every argument imaginable was used to convince her that she NEEDED to eat her food. Finally (as a last resort), she was told, "All of the poor Chinese children would LOVE to have this food that you don't want to eat."

To which Gail promptly replied, "SO? Give it to THEM!"

It was Easter Sunday. Robbie's family had gotten up, had their breakfast, dressed up, and gone to church.

Afterward, they went to Uncle Bob's for a gathering of the family for dinner. Walking into the house, little six-year-old Robbie stopped for a moment, looked all around, and made the statement: "We are ALL dressed up like human beings!"

This little five-and-a-half-year-old boy was sitting at the kitchen table with a pencil and paper. He asked his mother if he had spelled *cat* right. When she looked, she saw he had spelled it *cta*.

She said, "It should be *cat* . . . not *cta*."

He replied, "But, Mama, THIS cat was going to the BATH-ROOM!"

Four-year-old Ashley had an invisible friend. For two years Ashley made room for and included his friend, Sammy, in everything and every place he went, as well as talking to Sammy all of the time . . . and it was driving his daddy NUTS!

One day, while Ashley was in the backseat of their car and his daddy was driving, little Ashley started talking to Sammy. Ashley's daddy very angrily said, "ASHLEY! Now THAT is enough of THIS! You and I both know your FRIEND does NOT exist. Now, if I hear you say ONE more thing to him, I will stop this car and give YOU a spanking!"

Just a few minutes later, Ashley said, "No, Sammy! I can't talk to you now. Daddy's mad at us."

Ashley's daddy stopped the car, got out, pulled Ashley from the backseat, and gave him a spanking! When they were back on the road again, Ashley said, "See the trouble you got me in, Sammy?"

Daniel's mother made the remark that soon she wouldn't have any young children around, that the only babies would be those of her children. When her five-year-old son, Daniel, asked what she meant, he was told, "Someday, your two sisters will have babies, or you and your wife will have a baby."

Daniel replied, "I'M not gonna marry THEM!"

Four-year-old Mike had been sent to bed a couple of different times and, presumably, was asleep, but he didn't want to miss out on those great stories the grown-ups were telling.

When his dad looked up, there was little Mike, standing back, sort of in the shadows! His dad said, "MIKE! I told YOU to go to bed!"

Mike folded his little arms across his chest and angrily

stomped back to his bedroom while making the statement: "I'M getting SICK and TIRED of having to stay in bed ALL night long and getting ALL THIS SLEEP!"

Two-year-old Scott always put his most prized possessions on his riding toy and sat on them. Now, this worked very well for papers and small toys. . . . However, when his grandfather gave him a tomato from Grandpa's garden . . . UH-OH!

Two-year-old Crystal was asked by her grandmother, "Are you Grandma's girl, Crystal?"

To which little Crystal answered, in a quavering voice, "Almost!"

Little two-year-old Kevin had a VERY unique method of waving good-bye. He placed the knuckles of both of his hands up against his eyes, with his fingers covering the palms, and as he moved his fingers up and down, they became false eyelashes while he waved.

Mary (almost three years old) was in the kitchen with her dad. He was sitting at the table, making out a grocery list, (thinking out loud) as he wrote down the list of things that were needed from the store. When he couldn't think of anything else to add to the list, he asked, "What else do we need, Mary?"

Mary told him, "Go down to Safeway and get some dough!"

Two-year-old Jamie Sue had bitten her sister, Sarah. Their mother prompted, "Now, Jamie, what do you say to your sister?"

With no shame, Jamie bellowed, "WELCOME!"

His mother told four-year-old Ryan, "It is almost time to go pick Amy up at kindergarten. Put your shoes on, Ryan."

Little Ryan put his shoes on . . . on the wrong feet. Although she was busy in the kitchen, his mother noticed and said, "You have your shoes on the wrong feet, Ryan."

Ryan answered in an argumentative voice, "No, I haven't!"

"RYAN! You have your shoes on the wrong feet! Put them on right . . . RIGHT NOW!" his mother demanded.

To which little Ryan started crying, very hard.

His mother asked, "What's wrong with you, honey?"

Sobbing, Ryan answered, "They're the ONLY feet I've got!"

Right from the very start (from the time that she had been brought home from the hospital), Teresa had been an exceptionally GOOD baby, a very quiet and happy child. Yes, a sweet, lovable little girl.

One evening, she climbed up into her father's lap, telling him, "Daddy, tomorrow I'm going to be DIFFERENT!"

The following morning (her fifth birthday), and from then on, little Teresa WAS different . . . just like turning a page in a book . . . talk, talk, talk! Talk, talk, talk!

As all farmers know, a mouse in the house is nothing unusual. To some city folks, however, it can be a different story.

One day, while visiting at his grandparents' farm, four-year-old Richard saw a mouse run across his grandmother's kitchen floor. Since he lived in the city, he was not used to this and got excited, crying out, "Oh, Gwamma . . . look at the little WAB-BITT!"

Eight-year-old Phillip is a big help to his grandparents. His mother has a job and doesn't get home until after 5:00 P.M., so Phillip rides the school bus to his grandparents' house, staying there until his mother stops by for him on her way home from work. During his time there at his grandparents' house, Phillip answers the telephone and door, taking messages.

One day, his grandmother's birthday, a lady stopped by, leaving a beautiful heather plant. The lady was a very small lady, weighing (maybe) ninety-six pounds, was ten years older than his grandmother, and had been his grandmother's secretary a few years before. But Phillip didn't know all of this.

When his grandmother came home and saw the beautiful plant, she asked, "Who left this beautiful plant, Phillip?"

Phillip didn't know the lady but described her as being "a little girl with a lot of wrinkles!"

The grandmother was looking out the window at the chickens running around out in the yard and commented, "Look at those crazy chickens. They're so dumb, they don't know that chickens are SUPPOSED to ROOST when the sun sets."

Eight-year-old Tashua disagreed, telling her grandmother, "They aren't so dumb, Grandma. They know when the night crawlers come out!"

Eight-year-old Harvey was out in the potato field, scattering the sacks that would be used in harvesting the potatoes. As he walked along, he spotted a little field mouse. Harvey took off after the mouse, trying to step on it.

Very quickly, however, Harvey decided THAT wasn't such a good idea, when all at once the mouse jumped up onto his foot and on up his leg (inside his pants), clawing and scratching its way up one leg and down the other! Harvey took off for the house!

Her father was down, on an eye-to-eye level, having a serious talk with two-year-old Jamie Sue about her pottying in her pants. Little Jamie stood very stiff and sober through it all and promised, "I won't do that anymoell [anymore], Daddy."

He went on and on, however, until she brought him to a screeching halt by muttering, "Well . . . 'scuse me for livin'!"

63

Mandy's mother stopped in to pick two-year-old Mandy up from the preschool day-watch center. In the car, a short time later, she asked, "How did things go at school today, Mandy?"

Mandy didn't answer.

After waiting a short time, again her mother asked, "How did things go at school today, Mandy?"

Little Mandy answered (quickly, this time), "I don't want to talk about it!"

Two-year-old Jamie Sue had watched the Easter Bunny at the Oak Park Mall in Kansas City holding baby after crying baby. Finally, she wondered to Mommy, "The Easter Bunny don't BITE little girls, does he?"

A small boy was eating lunch with his grandmother at her house. His plate was still pretty full when, all of a sudden, he asked, "Can I have a hug, Grandma?"

Instantly wary of what was coming next . . . his grandmother gave him a hug. Then, very sweetly, he asked, "Can I go outside and give Freddy [her cat] a hug now, Grandma?"

Five-year-old Conley and his dad had gone fishing at the American Falls Reservoir, in southeastern Idaho. The reservoir is a very popular fishing spot, and like little Conley and his dad, many others were spending the night there.

Having slept in the back of their pickup, Conley woke up all bummed out to find his dad was fixing their breakfast of bacon and eggs. Upon hearing the negative comments by Conley, his dad had to explain, "Before we can eat FISH, Conley, FIRST, we have to catch some!"

Although there were a lot of fishermen there, no one was catching any, and it got to be pretty boring with everyone just sitting around with nothing happening.

Later in the day, Conley's dad broke out Conley's new pole, a thirteen-dollar Zebco (children's size) fishing pole, and threw the hook out into the water before handing the pole to Conley, and in a VERY short time, Conley had a bite! His very FIRST fish!

It soon became apparent that his fish must be a pretty good-sized one and that little Conley was having trouble landing his fish. He asked, "Dad, will you take my pole? This fish is pulling ME into the water!"

"Just turn around, put the pole over your shoulder, and walk up the bank, Conley," his dad directed.

Conley followed his dad's instructions and landed a big five-pound trout!

It was about eleven o'clock that night when the two happy fishermen walked into the house and little Conley proudly asked his mother, who was waiting up for them, "Mom, will ya cook my fish? I'm HUNGRY!"

Five-year-old Hillary asked, "Mommy, is Gosh God's wife?"

Surprised, her mother answered, "No, Hillary. What makes you think that?"

"Well," Hillary explained, "I hear some people say God, and some people say Gosh, and I don't know WHO Gosh is!"

Twelve-year-old Serenity was spending the weekend with her grandparents at their house. Her grandmother, having recently joined a small local writers' group, was reading some poems that had been written by her new poetic friend, Bob.

Serenity was reading Bob's poems, too. All of a sudden, Serenity exclaimed, "WOW! I wish MY writing was this neat! I just don't know HOW he can write so PERFECT! My teacher should see HIS handwriting!"

It wasn't Bob's handwriting, however. It was the SCRIPT-TYPE of his typewriter!

Eleven-year-old David and his ten-year-old brother, Eric, were always in trouble at church. One Sunday, they were acting up (as usual) and were told that since they hadn't behaved themselves, they were going to have to go down to see the pastor.

On their way to see the pastor, the boys were discussing the reason WHY they should have to go see him. Between them, they decided that if things started looking very bad for them, they would just take off.

David was the first one to go in. The pastor, seeing an opportunity to teach reverence for God's house, asked, "Where is God, David?"

All of a sudden, David jumped up, ran out the door, and grabbed Eric, and the two boys ran away! Running down the street, Eric wanted to know, "What happened, David?"

A worried David answered, "God is missing and they are trying to blame US!"

———————

When the CB radios first started coming on the market, ten-year-old Leo's parents were among the first to have one in their car. One day, Leo heard someone start a conversation on the CB radio. After giving the call letters, the person asked, "You got your ears on?" Pulling on his ears, Leo answered, "I've got MINE on!"

———————

One of the teachers was walking down the hallway at school. A little second-grade boy caught up with her, telling her about the substitute teacher in his room.

Breathlessly he said, "We have a new teacher in OUR room!"

"Oh . . . you have a new teacher? Who is it?" she asked.

"I don't know." He went on to explain, "But she has OLD hair!"

———————

While at the annual union picnic, the family was sharing a picnic table with some friends, and a discussion of nationalities was taking place at their table.

66

"We're Swedish and Danish," their friends claimed.

Seven-and-a-half-year-old Tony was listening as his mother proudly explained, "I'm English, German, Irish, Scotch, and Indian. And my husband is mostly Swedish."

All of a sudden, Tony blurted out, "MOTHER! You know what that makes us? We're MONGRELS!"

Dustin's mother was preparing to leave on a shopping trip to Coeur d'Alene, Idaho. Seven-year-old Dustin was busy giving her a last-minute list of the things that he wanted her to buy for him: "Buy me this, and this, and THIS, and—"

His mother laughingly answered, "I'm not going over to buy anything today, Dustin. I'm just going window-shopping."

"WINDOW-shopping? Well . . . then, Mom, you had better get upstairs and measure that window that Heath [Dustin's three-year-old brother] broke, so you can get the right size!"

When three-year-old Tristen would fall down, get bumped, or hurt herself slightly, her bottom lip would come out (along with the tears).

While holding his arms open, her father asked, "Ah-h-h . . . do you want some sympathy?"

Little Tristan came, got a big hug and kiss, then said, "I didn't get no sympathy, Daddy!"

Three-year-old B.J. had asked his mother if he could feed his new baby sister a cookie.

With a smile, his mother answered, "No, B.J."

B.J. wanted to know, "Why not?"

To which his mother answered, "Because she doesn't have any teeth."

"Well, Mom, we can go BUY her some teeth!" B.J. reasoned.

One of the swans in Manito Park in Spokane, Washington, liked to nip at the toes of the park's visitors. One particularly little three-year-old girl's toes seemed to be especially enticing to the swan.

The little girl's grandmother had quite a job, narrowly rescuing her granddaughter time after time. As a last resort, she simply picked her granddaughter up and carried her.

To which her granddaughter tearfully proclaimed, "But I WANTED it to bite my toe, Grammy!"

At three-and-a-half-years of age, Dick had a problem pronouncing some words. One of his well-remembered expressions is "I'll det my tap and tote, and doe out-tide" (I'll get my cap and coat and go outside).

Author's note: I have tried to keep most of the stories in my book humorous, on the light side. In the following story, however, though the topic is sad, the way these children rationalize the deaths of two elderly members of their family I believe makes this a story worthy of my book.

These children had recently lost their grandfather (after two years of watching him suffer considerably) and had, more recently, lost their great-aunt, Phyllis (suddenly, in a fire in her home).

Aunt Phyllis had requested that at her death her body be donated to science. In the event science couldn't use her body, her body was to be cremated and her ashes scattered over Puget Sound. This last, however, had not taken place immediately after her body had been cremated, due to the family's just putting it off.

After Palm Sunday services were over, the family decided to have dinner on their way home from church, but, FIRST they needed to stop and pick up Aunt Phyllis's remains. Thus, upon stopping, Dad took little Ricky with him and left the other five children in the car with their mother (baby Betsy, asleep on their mother's lap in the front seat and the other four sitting in the back seat).

Keeping in mind it was Palm Sunday (with Father George's sermon), as well as thinking about the recent deaths of their grandfather and their Aunt Phyllis, it was a pretty somber discussion taking place in the backseat of the family car.

Eleven-year-old Ellie wanted to know, "Where's Dad? Why is he taking so long?"

To which her mother answered, "Because he is picking up Aunt Phyllis's remains." She then went on to explain their Aunt Phyllis's wishes.

Ellie thought about it for a little while before saying, "When I die, I would like to be cremated and have MY ashes scattered over the mountains."

Her brother, seven-year-old Benjamin, agreed, "Yeah . . . me, too. I'd like to be spread out over the mountains, 'cause I don't want the fish to eat me, and I don't want the worms to eat me!"

To which their nine-year-old brother, Jesse, disagreed, stating, "I don't want anyone to burn me. . . . That's AWFUL! I want to be buried in the ground. If the worms eat me, it's better than being BURNED!"

Their little five-year-old sister, Daisy, told everyone, "I don't want to be burned, and I don't want worms to eat me. . . . I'M going to HEAVEN!"

Then, the subject changed slightly when Ellie said, "I think I'D rather die than suffer."

Benjamin: "I don't want to suffer, either. I'd rather just die."

Jesse reasoned, "I think I'd rather suffer, because, when I suffer, maybe someone will come up with a cure. And, then, I won't HAVE to die!"

Daisy decided, "I'll take die," causing Ellie to ask her little sister, "Well, Daisy, why do you say that?"

To which Daisy calmly answered, "Because I don't know what suffer means!"

———————

Five-year-old Daisy, her sister, eighteen-month-old Betsy,

and their mother were home alone. Mom decided for the three of them to take a nice long, relaxing bath together.

Later, however, Mom realized that she hadn't gotten their bath towels laid out first. She asked, "DAISY! How could YOU let ME get in the bathtub without our towels?"

To which Daisy answered, "Now, Mommy, you don't NEED towels in the BATHTUB!"

When Jean asked little Annie, "Where do you live?" little Annie replied, "In a house."

The family decided to practice for their good behavior in a nice café at some future time. One evening, they prepared and enjoyed a beautiful formal, candlelit dinner at home. Everything went very smoothly.

The meal was almost over and the family was still seated around the table. Terrie, complimenting three-year-old Autumn's table manners, "You sure are a good girl, Autumn."

Not wanting to be left out, five-year-old Daniel asked, "What about me?"

To which Russ replied, "I don't think YOU would make a very good girl, Daniel!"

While giggling, Daniel said, "I MEANT a good BOY!"

About herself, little Autumn added, "HER a good boy!"

After quite a struggle, his mother and father had finally convinced three-year-old Christopher to give up his bottle and had also gotten him potty-trained. Yep . . . Chris was a BIG boy now.

Later, he was on a trip to California with his grandparents and they had stopped at a rest stop. His grandmother had taken Chris into the rest room with her.

When they came out, little Chris was swinging his arms, rubbing both hands back and forth on his hips, and (obviously very proud) told his waiting grandfather, in a very loud voice, "BOY, oh BOY, Grandpa! I sure had a ker-splasher, THAT time!"

On Christmas Day, three-year-old Sarah was begging her Uncle Frank for a story.

"How about 'Little Red Riding Hood'?" he asked.

"Is that the one with the girl and the big bad wolf?" Sarah asked. "Forget it. . . . I know all about THAT one!"

Six-year-old Jessica had a problem learning to read. One evening, while working hard on a reading assignment, she came to a word she didn't know and couldn't figure out.

In trying to help Jessica figure out the word, Jessica's mother pulled a mother's no-no. She couldn't see the word on the page because of Jessica's bent head and, becoming frustrated, said, "Let ME have the book, Jessica. You can't read, anyway!"

The following day, while making cookies with Jessica, her mother asked, "Jessica, would you check the recipe and tell me what comes next? I think it's an egg, and that's spelled E-G-G."

Her little nose went up in the air as Jessica quickly retorted, "I don't know why you want ME to look for you. YOU said I can't read, anyway!"

Author's note: In 1954–55, my husband was in the U.S. Army, stationed in Lagendiebach, Germany. Our small daughter, Sandra, and I had the pleasure of being there with him. While there, we noticed that it was not an unusual sight to see a German male (young or old) stopped alongside a roadway urinating. The people there just didn't pay much attention.

One day, a German mother, Amy, was at a train depot with her three young children. While they were waiting there, they watched as a drunken man was staggering along beside the railroad tracks.

71

The man was having a terrible time staying upright. All of a sudden, he stopped. It soon became obvious that he was trying to urinate; however, because he was SO drunk, he was having trouble.

Amy's six-year-old daughter (having had much experience in helping her two younger brothers become potty-trained) became alarmed and frantically told her mother, "Mommy! Mommy! Why don't YOU help him? He cannot do it by himself!"

At the supper table, two-year-old David decided that he was full. His father instructed, "Finish eating your supper, David."

Little David insisted, "I'm full."

Later, when dessert (ice cream) was being dished out, David wanted some, causing his father to comment, "I thought you were full."

David, while pointing at his supper plate, said, "I'm just full of THAT!"

It was the night before Sarah's birthday. Tucking her into bed, her father told her, "Get to sleep, Sarah. Tomorrow is your birthday and you'll have lots of surprises."

Little Sarah asked, "What 'prises?"

Her father answered, "It's a secret."

"Oh, you can tell ME!" Sarah exclaimed. "I won't tell any-body!"

The little, round Ninja Turtles were the favorite toy of three-and-a-half-year-old Chuck. In fact, he had been known to load his pockets, his pant legs, AND his shorts with them, as if they were his concealed weapons, then stalk stiff-legged into the middle of the room, proclaiming himself, "NINJA TURTLE!"

Now, his little brother, two-year-old Mike, also gave a pretty good Ninja Turtle impression, stalking stiff-legged into the middle of the room, proclaiming himself, "TWIRTLE! TWIRTLE!"

The (little) big sister, two-and-three-quarter-year-old Sarah, took off her own slightly wet panties and put them on over her one-year-old sister Jamie Sue's diaper, so it looked like Jamie did it!

Five-year-old Matthew was getting restless as he waited for the church sermon to end. Sitting next to Millie, a friend of the family, he nudged her with his elbow to get her attention, telling her, "Millie, I need to go to the bathroom!"

Millie told him, "No, you don't, Matthew!"

To which Matthew responded, "How do YOU know if I have to go or not, Millie?"

Millie explained, "Because you went to the bathroom at MY house, before we came to church. Remember? I flushed the toilet for you. . . . THAT'S how I know."

Matthew gave her a dirty look that showed her he knew he had been caught in THAT one. But he settled down for a little while.

About eight minutes before the service was over, he nudged Millie again. "Millie," he said, "I REALLY need to go to the bathroom. I can't wait much longer."

Millie answered, "Well, try to wait just five more minutes, Matthew. Then, church will be over and we will be dismissed. You can go then."

While holding his two index fingers about an inch and a half apart, little Matthew commented, "Well . . . I MIGHT be able to wait THIS much longer!"

It was the middle of the winter in northern Idaho. The family was returning home in their nice, warm car. Their sacks of groceries were stacked in the backseat, and the sun was shining in through the back windows onto the sacks of groceries.

All of a sudden, there was a VERY loud POP! The car was stopped, to be checked for a blowout. None was found, however.

After checking things to find out what had caused the loud pop, it was found that the heat (inside the car), along with the sunshine, had caused the can of Pillsbury frozen rolls to expand.

With the TV advertisements of Pillsbury's cute little Doughboy in mind, seven-year-old Cynthia excitedly claimed, "I get the Doughboy! I get the Doughboy!"

Three-year-old Billy was the youngest child in a family with eight children.

One day, their mother put some of her delicious fresh homemade apple jelly on the table, with the strict instructions: "Now, each one of you is limited to two spoonfuls of jelly, EACH!"

The kids were all anxiously waiting to get at that jelly. Each one of them would carefully dip out the jelly (trying to keep as much jelly as possible on that spoon), all of them counting, "One spoon, two spoons," and then pass the jar on down to the next one. Then, the same process was repeated.

When the jar of jelly got to little Billy, however, he started dipping . . . one, two, three, four spoons of jelly onto his plate just as fast as he could, with an over-the-shoulder comment: "We ALL know I can't count!"

Three-year-old Debbie was helping her mother make the bed. When Debbie saw a corner of the sheet showing beneath the bedspread, she told her mother, "Mommy, the bed's petticoat is showing!"

Three-and-a-half-year-old Nicholas was staying at his grandmother's house.

She had gone into the bathroom to clean her dentures. After cleaning them, she put her teeth back into her mouth.

Little Nicholas was watching, and as she put her teeth into her mouth, he cried out, "OH! Grandma, PLEASE don't eat your TEETH!"

Getting into her Easter finery, three-year-old Jamie exclaimed, "I look like a CELEBRATION!"

Nine-year-old Spud liked to hunt groundhogs (he called them ground-DOGS) with his BB gun. When someone told him that groundhog hides were worth ten dollars apiece, young Spud thought that he was going to make some money!

One evening, when his dad came in from work, a very excited Spud met him at the door with the news: "I got me a GROUND-DOG, Dad! I did! I got me a ground-dog, and now I want my ten dollars!"

However, Spud was unable to convince his dad that the once fluffy but now wet, muddy, and filthy pillow made from an imitation-hair material that Spud had found, shot, and brought home was one of his ground-dogs! But he tried!

There is no doubt about it . . . television advertisements DO make their point.

Remember the American Cancer Association's advertisement: "It's a matter of life and breath," warning all of us of the dangers of smoking? Nine-year-old Deanna had watched this advertisement a number of times on television. One day, as she watched her uncle start to light his cigarette, Deanna gasped, "Uncle BOB! You won't have any BREATH!"

A third-grader, Jesse, was introduced to the multiplication tables. Evidently, they must have overwhelmed him, as he was sort of slow to start working at learning them.

One evening, Jesse's mother sat down with him and was pointing out, "They really aren't so tough, Jesse. Look . . . zero times ANY number is STILL zero, and one times any number is THAT number, and two times any number is THAT number

DOUBLED. That doesn't leave very many for you to learn, Jesse, just the threes, fours, fives, and—"

Jesse broke in with, "And I already KNOW the sixes, 'cause we have six kids here, and we have to split EVERYTHING six ways!"

Because of the fact that four-year-old Darrin's mother had sugar diabetes and sometimes suffered serious complications caused by this illness, little Darrin had been trained to dial the 911 emergency number.

While at his grandmother's house one day, Darrin walked into the room just as his grandmother was ripping off (for the THIRD time!) the turtleneck from the sweatshirt she was making and heard her say to herself, in frustration, "If I have to rip this out ONE more time, I'm going to throw myself down and bump my head on the floor a couple of times!"

She then looked up to see little Darrin standing there, and he told her, "Well . . . I WON'T dial 911 for YOU, Grandma!"

Four-year-old Starr was visiting her aunt. It was something Starr normally loved to do. This time, however, as she watched her mother's car disappear around the corner, it became evident that Starr wanted to go back home.

Starr told her aunt, "I want you to take me home. Now."

Being busy, her aunt told Starr, "No. I can't take you home right now, Starr; I'm busy."

To which Starr said, "But I want to go, NOW!"

"Well . . . then GO," her aunt told her.

Starr asked, "How can I get there?"

"WALK!" was the quick reply.

Little Starr went over to the cabinets and climbed up on one of the bar stools. While sitting there, swinging one of her legs back and forth in an agitated manner (to let her aunt know that she was angry), she asked, "Do YOU have a driver's license?"

"Why, SURE! Why?" Starr's aunt wanted to know.

With a very serious expression on her face, Starr answered, "I wanted to borrow it, so I won't have to WALK home!"

Four-year-old Scott was asked, "What is in your head?"
"My brain."
What does it do?" he was asked.
"It keeps my head warm!"

The six-year-old boy was having his eyes examined and was sitting in the chair of the phoropter, the machine that the Pinehurst, Idaho, optometrist used to check the curvature of the eyes.

Calling the boy by name, Dr. Vester instructed, "Open wide, now." Not being able to see anything, however, he repeated the instructions, "Come on, now . . . open wide." STILL not being able to see anything, Dr. Vester stepped back and looked around the corner of the machine at the boy in the chair, to find him with both eyes squeezed tightly shut and his MOUTH wide open!

The little first-grade girl came home after her first day of school. Her mother asked, "How do you like school, honey? Did you learn anything?"

"Yes, Mommy. Mommy, do you know what makes the ocean roar?"

After thinking about it for a few minutes, her mother said, "No . . . I don't know. Do you?"

"Well, Mommy, if YOU had all those crabs on YOUR bottom, YOU'D roar, TOO!"

Her mother thought, *Oh, NO! The FIRST day of FIRST grade! TWELVE more years to go!*

Six-year-old Jimmy's stepgrandfather had died. After the

funeral, the family was in the cemetery for the grave-side rites. Jimmy decided to wander off and look around.

Some distance away, Jimmy saw another open grave (which was being readied for another burial). He came running back to the family, still gathered around his grandpa's grave, just screaming and yelling, "One of THEM got OUT! One of them got AWAY!"

During a Sunday morning thunderstorm, after a loud clap of thunder four-year-old Sarah reassured everyone, "THAT'S Jesus and the 'ciples, bowling!"

Three-year-old Ricky (short for Fredrick) had a terrible time making himself understood, due to a developmental speech problem. He was going to a language preschool (speech therapy) in Tacoma, Washington, by way of a tiny school bus.

Ricky was usually home from school by 11:35 A.M. and no later than 12:00 noon. But . . . one day, he wasn't. He wasn't home by 12:00 noon and STILL not home by 12:15 P.M.

Since Ricky was only three years old, his mother was very worried (to say the least!) and called his school to ask, "What has happened to my little boy? Has Ricky been put on the bus yet? He isn't home!"

After they checked, they told her, "Yes, Ricky has been put on the bus and he SHOULD be home by now. But . . . hold on. . . . I'll contact the driver."

It took quite a while, and THIS is what his mother was told had happened:

"Today we had a new substitute bus driver for the returning children. Not knowing any of the children by name or face, the new driver used a list, with a child's first name listed next to his street address. After buckling the children into their seats, the driver looked at the list and, noticing there were more names on the list than there were children on the bus, called out the listed children's names. When called, the child would answer, or raise his hand, indicating he was there.

"When the name Frederick was called, little Ricky, not recognizing his name, kept quiet. The new bus driver assumed that Frederick, Ricky, was one of those absent children and did not stop by Ricky's house, so little Ricky stayed on the bus while the other children were taken to their respective homes.

"Later, however, it became apparent to the bus driver that there was a little boy on the bus and the driver didn't know this little boy's name or where he lived. The driver asked, 'What is your name, son?' "

Remember Ricky's speech problem? "Little Ricky answered, 'Icky.'

"The driver worriedly thought, *Oh, NO! He's messed his PANTS!* Keeping calm, though, he told Ricky, 'That's okay, son. Your mother will take care of THAT when we get you home . . . but, FIRST, we have to find out where you live. What's your name, son?'

"Again, the answer: 'ICKY.' "

THAT is when the bus driver got the call from the school: "We have a call from a worried mother; she is on the line wanting to know if you have her little boy on your bus?"

WHEW!

(P.S. Now ask Ricky to tell you his name; you will hear a VERY rolled-out, "R-R-R-R-R-RICKY!")

———————

Three-and-a-half-year-old Sarah was learning to answer the telephone and take a message.

One evening, when the telephone rang, Sarah was instructed, "Take a message, Sarah, and tell them we'll call back."

In haste, little Sarah picked up the phone and blurted, "HI! Call them back. . . . Who is you are?" Then she hung up!

———————

Three-year-old Lori had gone to Sunday school and church for the first time in her life. When she got home, her grandfather asked, "Well . . . what did you think of church, Lori?"

Lori answered, "OH! It was BEAUTIFUL, Grandpa!"

"It was, huh? What was it like?" he asked.

79

"They sang beautiful songs to ME, Grandpa!"

"To YOU? Don't be silly! A LOT of people go to church," said her grandfather, "and they DIDN'T sing only to YOU!"

To which Lori stubbornly insisted, quickly saying, "Oh, yes, they did, Grandpa! They sang those songs only to ME!"

"What makes you think they were singing them to YOU?" her grandfather wanted to know.

"Because they kept singing, 'LORI, LORI, HALLELUJAH!' "

David was raised on a farm in Kentucky. His family lived on one farm; however, they kept their stock on another farm, about a quarter-mile from where they lived.

Twelve-year-old Dave and his cousin had the job of loading and hauling hay from one farm to the other farm and feeding the stock there.

Now, in Kentucky, it gets unbearably hot in the summertime, so after having fed the stock, the two VERY warm boys would stop on their way back home and go skinny-dippin' in the river. Since they couldn't be seen from the road, they felt safe. One day, though, the boys came up out of the cool water to find that SOMEONE had thrown their clothes way up into the branches of trees growing along the river!

Because AIDS has become such a terrible sex-related health problem, Mom and Dad (after MUCH thought and discussion between them) finally decided to wait no longer, to explain the facts of life to their twelve-year-old daughter, De-Ann, and their ten-year-old son, Aaron. Mom and Dad were pretty nervous, not sure exactly how and where to start.

Dad started out with: "Do you know there is a difference between girls and boys?"

"Oh, sure, Dad. We know all THAT stuff!" they told him.

"Well . . . tell me the difference between your mother and me."

To which young Aaron quickly answered, "Well, Dad . . . Mom has a bigger nose than you!"

End of lecture.

———————

Five-and-a-half-year-old Kathy Kaleen had been dressed up to look extra cute for the union picnic.

Later, after the picnic was over, her Uncle Bob was taking her home. While driving along, he paid his little niece a compliment: "My, you sure are a little cutie, Kathy."

To which she quickly and indignantly answered, "I am NOT Cutie! I am Kathy Kaleen!"

———————

At five-and-one-half years of age, Dub was an early riser, but he would usually manage to keep himself occupied and let his mother sleep.

One morning, however, his mother awoke to a rather strange sound of water sort of splashing, then Dub's giggling, about two minutes later another sort of splash of water, then Dub's giggling. After the third sort of splash and giggle, she opened her bedroom door and SPLASH! right into a puddle of water on the floor in front of her door!

Little Dub had just thrown another small amount of water upon the cat's feet and was giggling at the way the cat would back up and lift, then shake its paw ever so daintily.

———————

The family was new in California, and five-year-old Rose, her two brothers, and her two sisters had all been warned about California's poisonous rattlesnakes.

One morning, Rose went outside to ride her tricycle and found that a harmless garter snake had crawled up onto the pedals of her trike!

Just SURE it was one of those poisonous rattlesnakes she had been warned about, little Rose was absolutely terrified! Trembling from head to foot, she ran for the house, screaming for her mother: "It's a RATTLING SNAKE, Mommy! It's RATTLIN'! It's RATTLIN'!"

Unknown to little three-year-old Liam (short for William), an early afternoon Easter egg hunt had been scheduled in Roseland Park, Kansas, where he lived.

At lunchtime, his mother called, "Liam, come in and eat, now. After you eat, we'll get you cleaned up and then you can go down the street and hunt for Easter eggs!"

Liam ate his lunch and got cleaned up, but before leaving the house, he went into his bedroom and came out with a toy gun.

Surprised, his mother asked, "Liam, what on EARTH are you going to do with that gun?"

"Because, Mom," Liam said, "I MIGHT run into some bad eggs!"

Grandma B. was chewing some aspirin gum to help soothe her sore throat, and three-year-old Sarah wanted some, too.

"No, Sarah," her mother said. "No more gum."

"Grandma has some," Sarah argued.

"Your grandma needs it for her throat," Sarah's mother explained.

Little Sarah was quiet for a minute, then, in a small voice, said, "I got bumps!"

Three-year-old Brandon had gone into the Wardner Gift Shop in Wardner, Idaho. The little Wardner resident picked out the penny candy he wanted, then went up to pay the cashier for it.

"That will be twenty-five cents, Brandon," Mary Lou said, adding, "plus one cent to feed the governor!" (Her quaint way of telling Brandon about the sales tax.)

Little Brandon thought for a minute, then, cocking his head to one side, asked, "Why do you have to feed the governor, Mary Lou? He doesn't live here with you. . . . Chuck does!"

After doing a little chore, three-year-old Jamie Sue repri-
manded her mother, "You didn't THANK-YOU me yet!"

Years ago, it was quite a treat to get a haircut at a barber-
shop.

One day, four-year-old Johnny and his dad stopped in at
O'Keef's (a VERY busy place) to get their hair cut. While they
were waiting for their turn in the barber chair, little Johnny was
watching as a barber covered a man's face with the white shaving
cream and then started sharpening his razor on a long leather
strap, slapping the razor back and forth, back and forth, back
and forth. . . .

Little Johnny had been watching (intently) all of this activity
taking place, and when one of the barbers called out, "OK,
Johnny!" Johnny pulled back against his dad, and he would
NOT get into the barber chair! His dad grabbed Johnny by both
arms, to sit him down in the chair, but Johnny stiffened his legs
and simply would NOT sit down in that chair!

Later, when he was asked, "Why not, Johnny?" Johnny
answered, "I didn't want MY hair cut THAT way!"

The family was on a trip and getting close to Arkansas. The
month was July and it was EXTREMELY warm.

Four-year-old Molly was trying to convince her father,
"Please, Daddy! Please, PLEASE turn the car around and go
back to Wyoming?"

"Why, Molly?" her father asked. "Why do you want to go back
to Wyoming?"

To which the heavily perspiring little Molly quickly explained, "Because, Daddy, I'M about to MELT!"

A little black boy and his grandmother were walking along,
on a sidewalk in downtown Wallace, Idaho, when the little boy

spotted a white man with a long black beard. The boy stopped, intently watching the man for a few minutes, then boldly walked up to him, saying, "Hello, Santa Claus!"

The man looked down at the little guy and answered, "Why, hello there, little white boy!"

At three-and-one-half years of age, little Sarah was overheard singing a favorite tune:

"Row, row, row your boat
Gently down the stream. . . .
Merrily, merrily, merrily, merrily
Life is down the drain!"

Three-and-a-half-year-old Maury was being raised in a strict Baptist home, and absolutely no swearwords or using the Lord's name in vain was tolerated.

Little Maury had a friend, Howie. Now, Howie's personality was completely different from Maury's. In fact, exactly opposite, as Howie was almost always in some kind of trouble (usually a fight) and he was allowed to use slang, as well as swearwords.

One day, Maury was playing with his friend Howie. While Maury was there at Howie's house, Howie's mother gave Howie a haircut and then gave Maury a haircut, too.

Later, when Maury went home, he walked into the house SO proud of his new butch haircut (just like Howie's). Maury's father, however, was upset about it and gave Maury a spanking, causing little Maury to angrily tell his father, "DAD! I'm going to beat the ELLA out of you!"

While in the spaghetti aisle at Dillions in Kansas City, three-year-old Jamie Sue startled an older lady by asking, "Mom, where is your pancreas?" Her mother told her where it was; then Jamie asked, "Well, where is your kidneys?"

The lady walked up to Jamie and said, "You sure are smart, honey!"

Little Jamie nodded and said, "Yeah, and you know what I wanna be when I grow up?"

"What?" the lady asked.

"A, a . . . a LION TAMER!" Jamie said.

On a visit to the obstetrician with her mother, two-year-old Sarah jerked up her shirt as the doctor entered the room and announced, "I got baby in MY tummy, too!"

Two-and-a-half-year-old Casey was an avid TV watcher. No matter WHAT it was, as long as it was on television little Casey just LOVED it!

One day, at his grandmother's house, Casey was (naturally) watching television. His grandmother had a headache and went into the bathroom to get (and take) some aspirin. She looked up to see little Casey standing in the doorway, watching her.

His question to his grandmother, while holding his slightly cupped hands about four inches out from each side of his head: "Grandma, do you have a headache THIS big?"

Sometimes we grown-ups can learn something from listening to our young children.

Two-year-old Daisy was just learning how to talk and usually spoke in a normal tone of voice, EXCEPT when talking to her babydolls. Then, her voice would lift to a very high pitch and she would talk baby talk to them.

When questioned about this, Daisy explained, "THAT is my mommy voice."

Jamie Sue had specified that SHE wanted a drink that was NOT water.

Her mother prepared juice for Jamie and two-year-old Ben, Jamie's little brother. Handing them their cups of juice, she said, "Now, this is NOT water."

Little Ben gulped his juice down and handed back his cup, "Moy [more] NOT water!" he gasped.

Whenever three-year-old Rhonda is riding past a wrecking yard with her mother, little Rhonda looks at the wrecked cars, there within the yard, and sadly tells her mother, "Look, Mommy, they are all dead."

Three-year-old Teresa's father liked to sit in his recliner late at night and watch television, while the household was quiet. She would get up and go sit on her dad's lap for a short time, watching TV with her dad, then play quietly on the floor in the light of the television set.

One night (or early morning), Teresa's dad came out of his bedroom to find her playing quietly on the living room floor in the light of the television, which she had turned on! He angrily said, "Teresa, if you don't stop coming out here in the middle of the night all by yourself like this, I'm going to get a rope and tie you in your crib!"

Later, upon seeing a coil of large rope that her dad had thrown into a corner behind his chair, little Teresa worriedly asked, "Mommy, is THAT the rope Daddy is going to tie me in my crib with?"

Three-year-old Jamie Sue, her sister, four-and-a-half-year-old Sarah, and their mother had stopped at a garage sale.

Sarah mentioned that she was looking for Barbie dolls (and clothes), and her mother told her that this was an old lady's sale and the lady probably wouldn't have any.

As they walked through the garage door, little Jamie in a loud, clear voice said, "THIS is an OLD LADIES' sale, isn't it, Mom?"

Her Aunt Janice was taking four-and-a-half-year-old Sarah with her on some errands, and Sarah's little sister, Jamie Sue, wanted to go, too.

Sarah exclaimed, "NO! Mama say we don't take her out in public!"

Art's mother had always been VERY strict with little Art's cleanliness, making sure he was washed and clean all the time.

One day, while Art and his mother were on a train (they were going to visit her parents), Art was very intently watching a Negro porter there on the train.

Now, four-year-old Art had never seen a Negro before, so he turned to his mother, asking, "Mommy, why didn't HIS mother make HIM wash?"

Little four-year-old Kim was the youngest in a family of seven children, and she was quite a tattletale. None of the other children could do ANYTHING without her running in to tattle!

One day, after the third story, her mother told her, "If you come in with just ONE more story, I'm going to give YOU a spanking!" Then she sent Kim back outside to play.

In a short time, however, Kim was back in the house, BUT with her lips pressed tightly together: "Mmmmm! Mmmmm!"

Her mother asked, "Are you trying to tattle again, Kim?"

Little Kim said, "No . . . I just want to TELL you something!"

When four-and-a-half-year-old Sarah asked, "Mama, what is the name of the cookies you and Jamie are making?" her mother answered, "They're called merrymaker cookies."

"Your name is not Mary," little Sarah told her. "You should call them Leanna-maker cookies!"

One day, while the seven-year-old boy was visiting with his grandmother, she asked him if he knew what labor was.

He thought about it for a minute, then said, "SURE! Labor is when a lady is having a baby!"

Seven-year-old Inge was talking with his friend, an elderly neighbor lady, about his hurt feelings resulting from not being invited to a neighbor girl's birthday party, since he and the girl were such close friends.

The elderly lady was trying to explain, "But maybe you SHOULDN'T have been there, Inge. Anyway, it WAS for girls only."

To which young Inge quickly answered, "Yes, I know about it being for girls only . . . but I SHOULD have been there!"

The second-grade teacher had asked, "What is yeast?"

Seven-year-old Jess (who had a speech impairment) answered. He pointed toward the east, stating, "That's yeast." Then, pointing in the opposite direction, toward the west, he said, "And that's vest."

Art's family was enjoying a day in Spokane's Manito Park.

A man there in the park was getting ready to take a picture of his wife. Having his wife sit on some boulders (on one side of a path) holding a bottle of beer, he went across the path (getting a little distance) to focus the camera and take her picture.

But seven-year-old Art walked between them just as the camera clicked and, turning around, told the man, "HEY! Don't take MY picture! I don't have no bottle of beer!"

One of those pretty metal cans of candy was on a shelf behind the glass doors of the hutch in the kitchen.

Her grandfather was sitting in his chair in front of the hutch when three-year-old Mari walked over to him and said, "I love you, Grandpa."

Smiling, her grandfather answered, "I love you, too, Mari."

Then, little Mari told him, "I smell CANDY, Grandpa!"

Two-and-a-half-year-old Jamie wasn't feeling very well, and her mother was rocking her. "Mommy, my things hurt."

"What hurts, honey?"

"My . . . my . . . FEELINGS!"

Three-year-old Rebakah, her older sister, and their grandmother were coming back from swimming at Little Diamond Lake, which is in the state of Washington.

Rebakah's sister and the girls' grandmother were talking about the different smells of wet hair and how wet hair smells like dog hair.

Little Rebakah wanted, very badly, to be in on the conversation; however, she couldn't think of ANYTHING that wet hair smelled like. That is, until they were almost home, when she said, "WELL! I just can't believe it!"

"Can't believe what, Rebakah?" her grandmother asked.

Rebakah answered, "I smell squirrel poop!"

Three-and-a-half-year-old Sarah was trying to run up the sliding board in her stocking feet. Being unsuccessful, she cried out, "OH! I wish I had bare-headed FEET!"

In an effort to keep four-year-old Daisy in a closer vicinity (on the same floor) while doing the housework, Daisy's mother sometimes permitted little Daisy to play with a dead telephone. This telephone, due to its not being needed, was kept unplugged and on a desk in the dining room of their Fircrest/Tacoma, Washington home.

During the summer while at her grandma and grandpa's in Idaho, little Daisy met and fell in love with a distant cousin, twelve-year-old Missy from Kansas City.

Later, after going back to her Fircrest/Tacoma home, Daisy would pretend to call and talk to her beloved Missy using this dead telephone quite often.

One evening, this Fircrest/Tacoma family was shocked and surprised to see a police car, with blue lights flashing, pull up on the street in front of their house and a policeman get out of the car and shine the beam of his flashlight through their living room window, then ring their doorbell and inquire, "What is going on here?"

What had happened was: When little Daisy complained to her older brother, "This telephone isn't working, Jesse. Will you fix it?"

Jesse plugged the phone in to get a dial tone; then he quickly unplugged it, not realizing that Daisy had had enough time to dial ANY number, let alone the 911 emergency number!

––––––––––––

On a drive through the country, two-and-a-half-year-old Jamie Sue had observed a cow pottying (urinating), in the field. Excitedly she asked, "THEY not in trouble, are they?"

––––––––––––

The (almost) three-year-old Jamie Sue was playing with her grandmother's Nativity set. While holding the angel next to the baby, Jesus, and speaking for the angel, little Jamie said, "Don't be afraid, Baby Jesus, 'cause I bring YOU good news!"

––––––––––––

While their mother was in the hospital, eight-year-old Edwin and his younger brother, five-year-old Matthew, were staying with Millie, a family friend.

Now, little Matthew liked to race. When he told Millie that he wanted to race, Millie told him to go outside and run around the house.

"But, Millie," Matthew said, "I want someone to race WITH!"

"Go talk with Edwin," Millie advised him.

When Matthew asked Edwin to race with him. Edwin said, "NO!"

"Why not?" Matthew wanted to know.

Edwin explained, "When we race, I always beat you and you always bawl . . . and I don't want to hear THAT, today!"

It was the first time that six-year-old Eric had played a Nintendo game. After Eric learned the basics of the game, it became obvious that he was enjoying himself, as he was overheard making the statement: "MY, oh MY! What a dinner we'll have tonight! What a feast! What a feast!"

Eight-year old Benjamin's homework assignment was to gather information on spiders. He had checked a book out of the school library and brought it home; however, he did not open the book up until the following morning.

His mother was very busy at fixing breakfast and lunch for Benjamin and his two brothers and two sisters, and she asked Benjamin to read aloud to Daisy, his little sister, which he did.

" 'The female black widow [spider] is much larger than the male," Benjamin read, and: " 'After mating, the female eats the male . . . ' " Benjamin stopped reading for a minute to comment, "Yeah . . . and she hardly even KNEW him!"

A very shy four-year-old Sarah had stood nearby while her little sister, two-and-a-half-year-old Jamie Sue, and their baby brother, eighteen-month-old Ben, sat on Santa's lap, and little Sarah had listened to Jamie tell Santa where she would be at Christmas.

Later, on the way home, Sarah's mother asked, "Did YOU tell Santa where YOU will be, Sarah?"

"Well . . . he knows I'm HER sister!" Sarah answered.

The family was enjoying a drive along one of Idaho's scenic mountain roads. A deer was seen, swimming across the river, and they quickly stopped the car, got out, and moved away from the car before snapping a picture of the deer in the river.

Later, when the film was developed, they received quite a surprise, for the developed picture showed not only a picture of that swimming deer (faint and faraway), but also a very clear (close-up) picture of little four-year-old Danny, standing in front of a HELP KEEP IDAHO GREEN sign, adding his own little stream of water!

In the small drive-in café in Wallace, Idaho, four-year-old Jolene went with her father to sit at the table to wait while her mother went up to the window to place their order, after which she went back to sit and wait with Jolene and her dad for their meal.

As she sat down in her chair, her mother made the comment, "Well . . . I've ordered."

To which little Jolene, while crossing her arms across her small chest, defiantly said, "THAT'S just GREAT! YOU order, but I don't get to eat!"

Their mother had given eleven-year-old Ellie and her little sister, five-year-old Daisy, some small pieces of candy. She gave Daisy the largest number (five pieces), with the instructions: "You learn to count these FIRST, Daisy. . . . THEN, you can eat them!"

Ellie had been working on her (own) math homework, but she decided to try to help Daisy learn how to count. Using Daisy's five small pieces of candy, Ellie would count, "One . . . two . . . three . . . four . . . five pieces!" When Daisy could count to five by herself, without a mistake, she took her candy to eat and Ellie went back to work on her own homework, popping a piece of her candy into her mouth to enjoy as she worked. This caused little Daisy to call out in a tattletale tone of voice, "MOMMY!

MOMMY! Ellie is eating HER candy, and SHE isn't supposed to yet . . . 'cause SHE isn't done with HER work yet!"

Bob's boss's son, five-year-old Tyler, told Bob, "I know YOUR name!"

To which Bob replied, "Oh, you do. . . . Well, what is it?"

Tyler said, "You're Bob Knox!"

Bob corrected him, saying, "No MY name is HARD Knocks!"

Tyler, with a puzzled look at first, then grinning, replied, "My daddy says that he is NEVER going to fire YOU!"

Bob was, naturally, pleased with this kind of talk. His supervisor, sitting there, listening to all of this, asked, "Well, what about me, Tyler? Is your daddy going to fire ME?"

Little Tyler answered, "I don't kno-OWE!"

Little Sarah was sick with mono and was "asleep" on the sofa in the living room.

In the kitchen, her little sister, Jamie Sue, sang her ABCs and Mommy and Daddy were praising her: "Good girl!"; "BOY! You know ALL of them, don't you?"; and "What a SMART girl you are!"

Suddenly, from the darkened living room, a weak voice was heard, "A . . . B . . . C . . . D . . . !"

While ten-year-old Jesse was filling out a Leggo order blank from a cereal box, he became confused at the wording. His mother was trying to help:

"What is your name, Jesse?" she asked.

"THAT was easy," was the quick reply.

"What month were you born?"

"December."

"What year were you born?" was the next question.

"Nineteen-eighty."

"And what is your birth date?"

"The twenty-eighth."

"Well . . . what is your problem, then?" his mother wanted to know.

"It says birthDAY! What DAY was it . . . Monday? Tuesday? OR WHAT?"

After many hours of tedious work, the ten-year-old Cub Scout completed his figurine, a beautiful replica of the Statue of Liberty, and Frank was VERY proud of his accomplishment.

Later, at the Blue and Gold Banquet, which was a big social celebration, lots of awards were handed out to deserving Cub Scouts. As Frank's figurine was being removed from the paper sack, poor Frank watched, horrified, as first the torch broke off, then her hand and an arm fell off. . . . His beautiful figurine, made of clay (which had hardened), absolutely crumbled!

Another Cub Scout, ten-year-old Andy, comforted his heartbroken friend, "No wonder she crumbled, Frank. After all, she gave birth to a NATION!"

Three-year-old Kimmy was standing next to her teenage Aunt Brenda, listening to her grandmother yelling at Brenda from the next room.

Evidently bothered, little Kimmy went into the next room to tell her grandmother to stop it.

Then, going back to Brenda, Kimmy cupped her hands over her mouth and, while giggling nervously, proudly told Brenda, "I told *Grandma* to STOP it!"

Three-and-a-half-year-old Daniel had been promised an ice cream cone by his grandmother, but FIRST he had to change his clothes and put his shoes on.

Daniel did. He put his shoes on (the wrong feet!), put a clean shirt on (backward!), and even put his clean jeans on (backward!), then came out telling his grandmother happily, "I'm ready, Grandma!"

After looking at him, his grandmother quickly admonished

him. "This won't do, Daniel," she said. "You have everything on backward; go back and do this right. Take your shirt off, turn it around, and put it on the right way. Take your jeans off, turn them around, and put them on the right way. And you have to put your shoes on the right feet!"

Little Daniel took his shoes off to change them around, then said, "Oh, Grandma, why don't YOU just turn ME around?"

As many people know, Jehovah's Witnesses do NOT believe in celebrating birthdays.

When a lady in a store asked four-year-old April (a little Jehovah's Witness girl), "How was your birthday party, April?"

Little April answered, "I don't know. . . . I didn't go!"

Back in 1947, before transistors, FM radios, or tape players had been invented, Harry, a Shoshone County, Idaho, teenager, eighteen years of age, invented and installed a record-playing system in the glove compartment of his car! This record player was capable of playing only one record at a time, utilizing the car's radio and speaker system.

A year later, Harry changed it, upgrading his record-playing system to a special heavy-duty automatic-changing record player (which was capable of holding and playing twelve 78 RPM records), and he installed this record player in the TRUNK of his car! The records could be preloaded on this record player (as the player was especially designed and built to hold these heavy records while the car was driven over rough roads and around sharp curves) then played at a later time, controlled from the dash of his parked car.

One evening, Harry and Donna were relaxing in his parked car, enjoying the Country and Western music (Harry's records) over the car radio. Harry wanted to surprise and impress his somewhat heavy-set girlfriend. "Donna," he said, "this next song is especially for you!" (He THOUGHT the following record would be "You're the Only Star in My Blue Heaven," by Gene Autry.) However, when the first words of the "Too Fat Polka" fell on their ears, Donna turned to a VERY surprised AND horrified Harry, telling him, "Gee . . . THANKS, Harry!"

Always curious, seven-year-old Benjamin had asked, "Mom, what does PG mean when they are talking about a movie on TV?"

His mother started to explain, "Parental Guidance—."

Benjamin's older brother, nine-year-old Jesse, interrupted. "NO!" he said. "PG means 'Pretty Good.' G means 'Good.' PG-13, means 'Pretty Good for thirteen-year-olds.' R means 'Rotten.' And X-R is 'Extra Rotten'!" Jesse explained.

Five-year-old Bozo, a little Jehovah's Witness boy, was a little on the energetic side. One Sunday, he was caught running in the Pinehurst, Idaho, Kingdom Hall and was chastened by one of the older men there. "Stop running in the Kingdom Hall, Bozo," Jim told him sternly.

While looking up into his face, Bozo asked, "Don't you love ME anymore, Jim?"

Baptism was the subject being discussed in the kindergarten class of the Pinehurst, Idaho Church of Latter Day Saints. The Sunday-school teacher asked, "Does anyone here know what *immersion* means?"

Five-year-old Jimmy quickly raised his hand, waving it frantically.

"Jimmy," she asked, "do YOU know what *immersion* means?"

"SURE," he said. "It means gettin' DUNKED down in the water and comin' up ALL clean!"

For some reason, Hakon had ALWAYS gotten "I'm hungry" mixed up with "I'm sleepy." Consequently, when he would tell his mother, "I'm sleepy," he was actually telling her that he wanted something to eat, and vice versa.

One afternoon, during a gathering in their home, eyebrows were raised when five-and-a-half-year-old Hakon told his mother that he was hungry and his mother answered, "I know, honey. You haven't had your NAP yet!"

The colorful pictures of flowers and bees on the material of the pretty dress three-year-old Sarah was wearing caused an older lady to ask teasingly, "Do those bees sting you, honey?"

To which little Sarah answered, "NO! They're not alive!"

In the kitchen, the grown-ups were sitting around the table, visiting with each other.

Eight-year-old Dorothy came in and flopped down in a chair, asking, "Mom, can I have a drink of water?"

Wondering why she couldn't get it for herself, Dorothy's frowning stepfather asked, "What's the matter with YOU?"

To which Dorothy quickly answered, "I'm THIRSTY!"

The backseat of their car was loaded with thirty-five airplane kits, glue, and two VERY excited brothers, eight-year-old Benjamin and ten-year-old Jesse (both talking, nonstop, to each other), as their parents were taking them to the school to join the other thirty-three Boy Scouts there to make model airplanes.

The sunshiny February day was beautiful, adding to the excitement while causing the boys' father to comment, "BOY! That sun sure is bright!"

Benjamin's face lit up, and he stopped talking to Jesse long enough to ask his dad, "Who? ME?"

Twelve-year-old Jennifer was spending the weekend with her grandparents at their house. Her grandfather was an inventor and stayed up late at night (sometimes all night) working on his different ideas.

He HAD been up all night, and when Jennifer arose early the next morning, she went into the living room to find him sitting in his chair, waiting for the chili and wieners to get hot enough to eat before he went to bed. "Jennifer, if you want some chili and wienies," he offered, "I have some heating up on the stove."

"CHILI?" Jennifer asked, astonished. "For BREAKFAST?" She then went on to say, "I'm strange, too, Grandpa . . . but not THAT strange!"

They were all at a family gathering at three-year-old Randall's Uncle Pat's house when Randall came into the room all covered with chocolate.

His mother really got excited (this wasn't THEIR house, after all!) and jumped all over the little guy, asking him, "HOW could you DO this? WHERE did you GET this? WHO gave you all this CANDY?" She was REALLY chewing him out!

His Uncle Pat, who had given him the chocolate candy, felt really bad about getting his nephew into trouble. In fact, he felt like sneaking out of his house!

Hanging his head down, little Randall pointed a chocolate-covered finger at his Uncle Pat and said sweetly, "It was the GOOD guy!"

When Danny was just a baby, he was found to have a defective heart.

Many times, Ann, an elderly good friend of the family, would come over to play with the bedfast Danny and give his mother free time for other things.

One of the most favorite times with Ann would be while petting the horses. Ann would carry little three-year-old Danny to the fence and tell him, "This white horse is the gentle one, Danny. You can pet the WHITE horse, but the black horse is NOT gentle. You canNOT pet the black horse." Every time Ann would give him the same instructions, and every time Danny would pet the gentle white horse.

One day, Ann was sitting near the window in Danny's bedroom. The sun was shining on her graying hair and Danny exclaimed, "Your hair sure is getting GENTLE, Ann!"

Three-year-old Nolan was sitting on his grandmother's lap. Looking up into her face (with its many deep laugh lines), little Nolan asked, "Why do you have so many cracks in your face, Grandma?"

Six-and-a-half-year-old Wayne and five-year-old LaMar are brothers.

Their mother was dismantling an old coat. This coat had a very strange-looking fur collar of a very bristly, stiff-looking material (maybe beaver fur or fox fur).

Their mother's sister, their aunt (who lived next door), got the idea for a prank. Taking the fur collar, she sewed on two buttons (for eyes); then she split an old white sheet into two pieces and attached them to each side of the fur collar, thus turning that fur collar into an animallike-looking THING, and put it underneath the boys' mother's clothesline.

Early the following morning, their mother took a basket of clothes out to hang them up and was VERY upset to see this animal thing lying there, looking up at her!

Rushing back into the house (with her STILL-FULL clothes basket), she instructed Wayne to go out and KILL it!

Wayne took a large stick out with him and proceeded to kill it . . . WHUMP! WHUMP! WHUMP! Over and over and over again. WHUMP! WHUMP! WHUMP! Finally, it caught on the end of his stick and was sent flying onto the roof of the nearby woodshed.

When Wayne went back into the house, he told his mother, "OK, Mom. I did it!"

Their mother then instructed little LaMar to climb up on the woodshed and check to make SURE it was dead!

Three-year-old Marcus had just been told, "When people die, they are buried in the dirt, in the ground."

You could see his brain working as he thought that over for several minutes. Remembering that his grandfather had told him that when you flush the toilet, it went into the ground, little Marcus expressed worry: "Will the dead people be in a sewer?"

It was six-year-old Billy's first day of school. Happily, he went to school (the first grade) in one of Idaho's small towns' schoolhouses.

At lunchtime, Billy went home for lunch, but he was NOT there for the afternoon class. His teacher was very concerned and asked the principal to call Billy's parents; however, they didn't have a telephone. The principal drove to Billy's house to find out what had happened to Billy.

Returning to school, the principal told the teacher that Billy's mother wanted to bring Billy over after school to talk to her. All afternoon, the teacher worriedly wondered, *What have I done wrong?*

After school had been dismissed, Billy and his mother came in and sat down.

His teacher asked, "Don't you like being in my room, Billy? Aren't you happy?"

To which Billy quickly replied, "Oh, yes! I love being in your room."

"Well . . . what is the problem, then?" she wanted to know.

"You see, I have wanted to be able to read for a long time. Everyone has been telling me, 'Just wait until you go to school, Billy, and you'll know how to read.' But," he said, "when I came to school this morning, I COULDN'T read. . . . I didn't know HOW!"

Grandma was walking around in the Pinehurst, Idaho,

Kingdom Hall with Tyler, her two-year-old grandson. Mari, her three-year-old granddaughter, wanted to walk with them, too.

When her grandmother said, "Yes," and started to walk in one direction, little Mari, however, wanted to walk in the opposite direction. Absolutely INSISTED, even.

"Why do you want to walk THAT way, Mari?" her grandmother asked.

Mari quickly answered, " 'Cause your purse is over here!"

Two-year-old Jason was being very stubborn about getting potty-trained.

One day, his grandmother stopped by to take Jason and his mother out for some pie and coffee and ice cream sodas for the children. She walked into the house to find little Jason was in the process of messing his pants. Upset, she asked, "Jason, why don't you tell your mom when you know you have to go?"

The very stubborn answer: "NO!" came from the little guy.

His grandmother told his mother (over Jason's head), "Why don't you take his messy shorts off and tie them around his head and make him wear them all day long? That's what I would do!"

Later, after getting things cleaned up and Jason's clothes changed, they went out and got into the car, little Jason climbing into the backseat with four-year-old Ryan, who was waiting in the car.

Shaking his finger at Ryan, Jason warned, "And, Ryan, you better not mess YOUR pants with Grandma around!"

Six-year-old Patty was in the first grade of a small Idaho town's school, and her mother was room mother for Patty's class.

During one of the PTA meetings, Patty's mother was serving refreshments and was wondering why some of the parents there were looking at her, then seem to be laughing sort of to themselves, under their breath. She wondered, that is, until she went into Patty's classroom.

There, written out on the blackboard, was: "Patty's daddy

went to sleep on their new davenport and burned a hole in it with his cigarette, and her mommy SURE was mad!"

Later, when she was asked to explain why that story was on the blackboard, little Patty said, "I forgot to take anything for show and tell!"

———————

Being a Cub Scout den mother, Georgia liked to take the boys on hikes in the woods and combine the hikes with a picnic when she could.

On one such hike, she had asked each of the boys to bring something from home for their picnic lunch, and she furnished the fried chicken. They were going to gather pinecones on their hike, so Georgia took her young son, three-year-old Mike, along with them.

They chose the spot, spread the blanket, and had their picnic, then went about collecting their pinecones. Later, when they were cleaning up the lunch paraphernalia and getting ready to go home, they realized they had spread the blanket (and had eaten their lunch) on top of a huge anthill! There were ants EVERYWHERE!

Georgia jokingly told the boys, "Oh well . . . you can't have a good picnic without ANTS!"

The next time the boys were to go on a picnic/hike, everyone was busy gathering up everything needed, and just as they were ready to leave the house, little Mike ran in, excitedly calling, "Mama! Mama! Did you get the ANTS?"

———————

Four-year-old Cindy and five-year-old Deanna were walking with their grandmother along one of the logging roads near Murray, Idaho.

A Forest Service brush crew (one of them a woman) was working along the roadside. With their tools, shovels, axes, and Pulaskis, as well as their hard hats and gloves, the crew did, indeed, resemble prospectors.

Deanna said, "Look at THAT, Cindy! One of THEM is a girl!"

causing little Cindy to answer, "Yeah . . . I know what SHE is. She's a PROSTITUTE!"

A VERY surprised grandmother asked, "WHAT did you say, Cindy?"

"Yeah . . . you know, Grandma," Cindy calmly explained, "Prostituting for gold . . . like they do on TV."

———————

Nine-and-a-half-year-old Rob had started playing baseball on the Dallas (Oregon) Minor team. He was to go on into the Intermediate team the following year. Rob was such a good player, however, they put him up (ahead of schedule) into the Intermediate team.

When the boys were asked to sell candy bars for their Babe Ruth uniforms, Rob was hitting the local business places and selling BOXES of candy bars!

Rob walked into one of the local taverns with his candy bars, causing the bartender to yell out, "Get out of here! You're not allowed in here. . . . You're just a minor! Get OUT of here!"

To which young Rob straightened his shoulders and haughtily stated, "I am NOT a Minor! I am INTERMEDIATE now!"

———————

After listening to her mother read the bedtime story, one-and-a-half-year-old Pam STILL wasn't ready to give up and go to sleep. As her mother turned the knob of the door to leave the bedroom, little Pam looked up from her crib to ask, "Now . . . will you tell me the COMMERCIAL?"

———————

In his act of heckling his mother, eleven-year-old James asked, "You know WHAT, Mom? You know what, Mom? You know WHAT?"

Finally, in frustration, she replied, "No . . . WHAT, James?"

"It took me all my life to get to be ELEVEN years old!" was his earth-shattering news!

———————

Instead of singing, "Bring the wandering ones to Jesus," little three-year-old Ethyl would sing, "Bring the ORNERY ones to Jesus!"

Grandma had stopped in for a visit. As she stepped through the door, little Teddy ran over, crying out, "Grandma! Grandma! Look-it my new pajamas, Grandma!"

After a brief inspection, Grandma gave the compliment: "BOY! Those are the cat's pajamas, Teddy!" causing little Teddy to turn on the tears. "It is NOT!" he argued. "It's MY pajamas!"

Seven-and-a-half-year-old Lauren was definitely NOT feeling well. She had an upset stomach, vomiting, etc., etc. It was assumed that Lauren had the flu. However, when she complained of hearing STATIC in her ears, she was taken in to see the doctor.

"I feel TERRIBLE!" Lauren said in answer to the good doctor's question. "I heard EVERYTHING . . . ALL NIGHT LONG! I heard the furnace come on and the dog drinking out of the toilet—"

"Well, that's not so bad, Lauren," the doctor said.

"Yeah . . . but I don't think it had been FLUSHED!"

A very excited three-year-old Jesse was telling his daddy, "I want to go see *Star Wars!*"

"I don't know where it's playing, Jesse."

"Yes, you DO, Daddy!" Jesse argued. "It says on TV it's playing in a theater near YOU!"

Living in the small town of Pinehurst, Idaho, ten-year-old Glen was easily recognized when he shot a hole in the neighbor's picture window with his BB gun. Naturally, she called the police, reporting him.

Since young Glen's name had been popping up a number of times in connection with other things (such as this), the police chief wanted to change the young fellow's ways. The police chief had a plan:

Escorted by the police commissioner, young Glen (with hands handcuffed behind his back) in the backseat of the police car, the chief drove around in the small town.

Stopping in front of a house, the chief asked the VERY subdued Glen, "Do you know who lives there?"

Glen mumbled his answer, causing the chief to demand in a very loud voice, "When I ask you a question, YOU answer me in a LOUD and CLEAR voice! Is THAT understood?"

"Y-y-yes, s-sir!" the intimidated Glen answered.

"Now . . . who lives in that house?"

In a much louder voice, Glen told the chief the name of the boy (a friend of his) living there.

After four such stops, requesting (and receiving) the names of boys living in the different houses, the chief commented to Glen, "You know every ornery brat in town, don't you?"

"I GUESS so," a very scared young Glen acknowledged.

———————

Three-and-a-half-year-old Katelynn and her three-year-old cousin, Justin, were to be part of a big wedding taking place in the near future, with Katelynn the flower girl and Justin the ring bearer.

Excitedly little Katelynn told her preschool teacher and classmates, "I'm going to be in a BIG wedding! I'm going to be the flower girl . . . and . . . you know my little cousin, Jason? He's going to be the . . . uh . . . uh . . . REINDEER!"

———————

While her mother and grandmother were fixing sandwiches for lunch, one-and-a-half-year-old Angie went with her grandfather to buy some french fries to bring home and eat with the sandwiches.

Setting the fries in the car seat alongside Angie, Grandpa

made the statement: "NOW, we can eat!" (Meaning later, of course.)

However, little Angie insisted, "NOT until after we PWAY [pray], Grandpa!"

———————

During a convention of Jehovah's Witnesses, a Negro man was seated next to Harold's mother.

Now, six-year-old Harold had never before seen a real live Negro, and the youth couldn't take his eyes off the man. Finally, he tentatively reached over and stroked the man's face. . . . "MOM! It doesn't come OFF! How come he doesn't wash the grease off?" came from the surprised Harold.

In return, the Negro man reached over and, and while rubbing Harold's face, retorted, "Well . . . HE ain't DONE yet!"

———————

Mom and Dad, with three of their seven children, were shopping at Sears. While there, Mom decided she would check on a cart on which they could place the heavy laser printer in their home office. After locating one, she (naturally) wanted Dad's opinion.

Along with seven-and-a-half-year-old Daisy, Dad looked it over, finding that it wasn't as sturdy as he felt they needed. He told the saleslady, "I'm sorry, but this isn't what we're looking for. We have a lot of rug rats at home, and I don't think this will do." He then turned and walked away.

Thinking her dad meant MICE, little Daisy told the saleslady, "Yes, and when we got back from vacation, we found THREE of them dead in the rug!"

———————

While driving by the display of headstones in Boston, Massachusetts, Julian's nanny was surprised to hear the little four-year-old comment, "I want a heart-shaped tombstone on MY grave."

While going past the same display the following day, little Julian stated, "I want to die!"

"Why do you want to die, Julian?" his nanny asked.

" 'Cause nobody knows what kind of clothes God wears!" was Julian's reason!

Ten-year-old Jesse and eight-year-old Benjamin were playing WHERE-IZ with their two-year-old sister, Betsy.

"Where is your nose, Betsy?" Jesse asked.

Little Betsy put her finger on her nose.

Benjamin asked, "Where is your ear?"

Betsy pointed to one of her ears.

"And, Betsy," Benjamin continued, "where is your belly button?"

She pulled her little shirt up and proudly pointed to her belly button.

But when Jesse asked, "Where is your brain, Betsy?" with a perplexed look on her face, she shrugged her little shoulders slightly and informed them, "GONE!"

Now, it's a well-known fact that Lonnie just LOVES pork chops.

Coming home from school one afternoon, the six-year-old Lonnie asked, "What's for supper, Mom?"

"Pork chops, mashed potatoes and gravy, peas, and a salad."

"Oh, GOOD, Mom!" Lonnie contended, "Why . . . you're the BEST Mom I EVER had!"

Grandma had made plans to get her elderly father and take him down to the local poolroom where he could visit with his old friends for an hour or two, while she, with her grandson and her sister, would go on downtown and have some ice cream.

Now, her father had had a number of small strokes, leaving him with the problem of controlling his kidneys and bowels.

Going into her father's house, Grandma noticed that he

smelled like his pants were full. In an extra sharp tone of voice, Grandma asked, "DAD! Did you mess your pants, again?"

Little three-year-old Danny was standing nearby and consoled his great-grandfather, "Don't be scared, Great-Grandpa! Grandma won't spank you. She don't spank me when I mess mine!"

Three-and-a-half-year-old April had been sick and running a high fever for some time. In order to get her to take her medicine, she was always told, "Take your medicine, April. You NEED it to make your fever go down."

One day, her fever went down. While pointing to her face, little April proudly and happily informed her mother, "My fever went down . . . ," then, while pointing in turn to her chest, stomach, legs, and feet, added, "down, down, down, down . . . to my TOES!"

Three-year-old Joshua wanted to draw a picture of himself showing his new haircut. First he drew his face, next the haircut, then a fat tummy.

"I'd better draw a heart in the stomach," he explained out loud to himself. "Then, I can love!"

Annie's pregnant mother was working a crossword puzzle. "With child," was the meaning of the word she needed, and it started with an *e*.

Her sister offered, "I have heard the word *enceinte* [pronouncing it "ENT-I-CET"] used for 'going to have a baby, being pregnant.' Maybe that is your word."

A short time later, Annie's grandmother brought in a large birthday cake, causing the compliment, "BOY! That sure does look enticing!"

When five-year-old Annie was offered a piece of her mother's birthday cake, she declined, worriedly stating, "No, I don't wanna get a baby!"

On a trip to Spokane, the kids were in the backseat of the car, discussing what they were going to do when they were grown-up and what they were going to buy when they got rich.

Going past some huge round metal storage tanks out in a field, little five-year-old Brent pointed to the tanks and stated, "I'm gonna buy me one of THOSE for my KOOL-AID!"

In the Tall Pine, a small café in Pinehurst, Idaho, a man had brought his young children in for ice cream cones. The following conversation was overheard:

"This Tall Pine has been here for a LONG time. It was here when I was a kid. Why . . . it must have been here for at LEAST one hundred years!"

His daughter (about five-and-one-half years old) said, "Aw-w, Daddy, you are not one hundred years old! You're only twenty-NINE!"

The oldest of the five boys, sixteen-year-old Mike, had already had quite a bit of experience in holding a baby and a baby's bottle, as well as changing diapers, thanks to his younger brothers.

And, then, baby Larry was born.

Not too long after returning home from the hospital, and having an errand to run, Mom and Dad asked Mike to baby-sit while they were gone. Lo and behold, right after they left, baby Larry's diaper needed to be changed!

Young Mike was absolutely horrified to find BLOOD in his infant brother's diaper!

What to do?! Mike knew he couldn't contact his parents, and as he didn't know what was causing the blood, the only thing Mike could think of to do was call an ambulance. This he did.

When the ambulance crew arrived, they checked, only to find that baby Larry had been circumcised. (The REASON for the blood!)

I might add that young Mike had a hard time living THIS down for YEARS to come!

———————

A mother's NO-NO had been pulled! In front of her young teenage daughter, Mom had made the comment: "It WOULD be nice to spend a day in the woods and get away from the kids."

Looking her mother straight in the eye, Serenity asked, "Why do you need to get away from us kids, Mom? Is there something WRONG with us?"

———————

Twelve-year-old Chris was in a fight. He called his dad on the telephone to ask, "Come and get me, Dad? I just can't seem to keep my hands off other people!"

———————

While his two young daughters, three-and-a-half- and two-and-a-half-year-old Allison, were playing with their toys in the bathtub, their father was visiting with his dad via telephone.

The telephone, being placed just a short distance from the bathroom door, allowed their father time to drain some water down, add hot water (thus warming it up), then go back to visiting with his dad. Several such warm-ups had taken place and the girls had spent a lot of fun time in the water.

All of a sudden, a piercing scream came from the bathroom! Instantly, dropping the telephone, their father raced into the bathroom, expecting the worst . . .

To find little Allison, holding up her water-wrinkled hands, crying out, "There are CREEPY CREATURES on my hands!"

———————

Two-year-old Danny had fallen and skinned his elbow. The tearful little fella came into the house requesting, "A ramb-Aid, for the owee on my bellbow?"

———————

At (almost) three years of age, little Abbey was very impressed with Christmas, with all of the fancy foods and candy, as well as Santa Claus and her gifts of dolls, games, and other toys.

While tucking little Abbey into bed Christmas Night, her mother asked, "Well, what do you think of Christmas, Abbey?"

After thinking for a short time, little Abbey stated, "I've decided Santa is a GOOD man!"

Terry's dad was up at his still (behind their house) in Virginia.

Six-year-old Terry was asked by a Revenue man, "Where is your dad? Do you know where he is?"

"Yes, sir," Terry answered. "He is up at the still."

"Do you know where his still is?" the Revenue man asked.

"It's about one hundred yards back up there," said Terry, while pointing up behind their house.

"Will you show me where that is?"

"Yes, sir . . . for five dollars, I'll take you right there," Terry offered.

"Okay, son. I'll give you the five dollars when we get back," the Revenue man promised.

"NO, SIR!" little Terry exclaimed. "You have to give it to me FIRST, 'cause when you go in THERE, you ain't coming BACK!"

Little Sis was about six years old when she had her ears pierced. While proudly showing off her newly pierced ears and new earrings to her friendly neighbors, Sis was teasingly told, "If you put holes in your ears, your TEETH will fall out!"

Lo and behold, in about two days, little Sis lost her first baby tooth!

Consequently, on her next visit to her friendly neighbors, they noticed that Sis was NOT wearing her pierced earrings!

Evidently entranced, six-year-old Harold was staring into

111

the eyes of the Negro girl. "Do you see everything in brown?" Harold wanted to know.

"Not unless YOU see everything in BLUE!" she retorted.

At the preschool day-care center, the two little girls (both about three-and-one-half years old) were standing face to face, Sally a poor little girl, seemingly in need of everything, including lots of love and affection, and Janie a well-dressed, uppity little lady.

Poor little Sally tried to kiss little Janie, causing the prissy little lady to push Sally away, while telling Sally, "I don't LIKE to be kissed."

Little Sally, then, tried to put her arms around Janie and give her a hug.

Again, little Janie pushed Sally away, telling her, "I don't like to be hugged."

After thinking about this for a couple of seconds, Sally shoved Janie, causing her to fall down and cry.

Going over to Janie, little Sally asked the tearful little lady, "OH! You don't like to be PUSHED, either?" She then turned and walked away.

The family was eating supper one evening during the Yuletide season. All of a sudden (out of the blue), little three-year-old Arv asked, "Daddy, did YOU see Joseph and Mary and their donkey go past?"

Three-year-old Megan was talking to her grandfather on the telephone, telling him about all of the places her family had gone and the many things she had seen while they were on their vacation trip to California.

"Did you have a good time on your vacation trip, Megan?" he asked.

"Yes, Grandpa," Megan answered, adding, "But . . . I 'ZAUSTED!"

An aria was being performed by the fifth-graders during the Christmas program of the Churchill School in Ottawa, Canada.

Robby, a member of the choir, was standing in the front row. The boy standing behind Robby thought it would be fun to poke Robby in the back. Robby turned, telling the boy sharply, "Quit it!"

Just a little later, the same thing happened, and again Robby turned, ordering the boy more sharply, "QUIT IT!"

The timing was perfect; the choir had just finished singing the line, "Peace on earth, goodwill to men . . . " and, poke! Young Robby turned and hit the boy right in the face with his fist!

With the palms of both of her hands turned up in frustration, eleven-year old Debbie wanted to know, "The cookie monster eats cookies; the boogyman boogies, so . . . what does the booger man do? Eat BOOGERS?!"

Nine-year-old Daniel and his two older sisters, Jennifer and Serenity, were spending a couple of days at Grandpa and Grandma's house.

Daniel had found a toy gun out in the yard and brought it in to show it off.

"Hey, Daniel . . . ," he was teased, "are you SURE that isn't a REAL gun?"

"We'll ask Serenity to look at it," the serious young Daniel answered. "SHE is in ROTC and SHE will know!"

The month was August. It had been a very trying day for Dad. He came home late from the new logging site, very hot, dirty, and extremely tired.

"Judy," he said to his wife, as she put his late supper on the table, "you'd never guess what those clowns did up there today!"

He then went on to explain, "Our new logging job has two

roads, a lower road and an upper road. The Forest Service wanted us to start logging the lower road first, as they had slash crews in a area just below OUR job piling limbs and cleaning up that previously logged-out site just below us. So, we moved the equipment in on the lower road, and started to work. We had about three or four decks of logs already. Today, those clowns, started a FIRE in one of those brush piles! The fire got away and came close to catching our men and equipment in that runaway fire! Why, if it hadn't been for our men and equipment, plus the fire-fighting tools and water truck there . . . they would have had EVERYTHING burned up! The fire burned into TWO of our log decks, anyway!"

About an hour later, while he was sitting in his chair, watching TV, and relaxing, a very quiet, subdued little Paula climbed into her father's lap. "Daddy, are there REALLY clowns up in the woods, starting fires?!" the worried little five-year-old asked.

While driving along one day, Dad started singing the famous Almond Joy and Mounds candy bar jingle about feeling like a nut.

Not to be outdone, from the backseat, to the same tune (changing the words slightly), five-year-old Ricky sang out, "Sometimes Dad feels like a nut. . . . Sometimes he don't. . . . "

Twenty-two-month-old Stephanie had found an open cabinet door under the sink and crawled in.

Upon seeing this, her mother started the warning count, "ONE . . . "

A high-pitched baby voice, "TWO . . . " was heard from under the sink, instantly followed by little Stephanie backing out!

Two-year-old Mica had been getting pretty antsy in the car. Trying to keep him entertained, Mom was singing "Old MacDonald Had a Farm" as she was driving the (approximate) twenty miles between Kingston and Wallace, Idaho.

By the time they were at the Wallace city limits, she was at her wits' end, trying to think of another farm animal to put into the song, but she just couldn't.

Then, looking over at Mica (to see if he looked like he was enjoying her song), she was very surprised to see him sitting in his car seat, his face up against the window of his door, and with BOTH hands over his ears!

Family friends were visiting at the home of Dina's parents. One family had been to France, and the other family had spent some time in Africa. The children of the visitors were singing French songs and African native songs and dances, both of which contained many *bon(s)* and *bong(s)*.

Not to be outdone, but not knowing anything to sing with a *bon* or a *bong*, little two-year-old Dina walked out into the center of the living room, then, with arms outstretched, started swaying and twirling around, singing, "Ohh . . . the Bon Marche . . . "

Jill's father is black and her mother is white; thus little Jill is a mulatto.

After divorcing Jill's father, her mother married a white man, and a baby boy was born to this couple.

Now, Jill's hair is soft, black, and curly. Her baby brother is white, and his hair is straight, blond, and fine.

One day, while in a local supermarket, four-year-old Jill was standing next to the shopping cart that her one-year-old brother was sitting in. Jill was patting and rubbing his straight blond hair. He, in turn, was patting her black curls. They made quite a sight, and people in the store would walk past them, then turn to stare at them.

Unaccustomed to seeing black people, one little girl (about four years old) walked past them, just staring. She turned around and walked slowly back past them, staring intently AT them. Then, turning again, she walked back to them. This time, she stopped and asked little Jill, "Are you a SHEEP?"

––––––––––––––

Referring to his sister, four-year-old Willis said, "SHE'S a girl and I'm a boy!"

"How do you know the difference, Willis?" his grandmother wanted to know.

Grinning broadly, the proud little Willis explained, " 'Cause . . . I have white hair!"

––––––––––––––

Four-year-old Breann's candid explanation for passing gas: "My BOTTOM burped!"

––––––––––––––

Four-year-old Justin's view: "Thanksgiving means THAT'S the time we tell Grandma, 'Thank you,' for fixing dinner . . . 'cause we forget all the rest of the time!"

––––––––––––––

Sometimes, a person doesn't catch the funnies in a joke and what transpires can be just as funny as the joke itself.

Eight-year-old Harold told his grandmother the following joke:

"McGregor of Scotland, James of England, and Murphy of Ireland were discussing the event of the Olympics that was happening right there where they lived. 'We want in to watch, but we don't have the money for the ticket,' was decided by all three men.

"Noticing that the participating athletes were being given free access into the arena, the three buddies decided to CLAIM to be athletes.

"So . . . McGregor, packing a telephone pole on his shoulder, told the ticket taker, 'McGregor, Scotland, pole-vaulting,' and was given free entry into the arena.

"James picked up a manhole cover from the street and,

carrying that up on his shoulder, claimed, 'James, England, discus throwing,' and was also given free entry.

"Poor Murphy couldn't think of anything to gain his own free entry until he spotted a roll of barb' wire in front of a hardware store. Gingerly shouldering that roll of barb' wire, Murphy proceeded to claim, 'Murphy, Ireland, fencing!' "

When Harold's grandmother couldn't catch the joke, young Harold explained, "GRANDMA! Murphy was out BARB'-WIR-ING!"

The Halloween costume being worn by the two little girls locked them together as one.

When they knocked at her door, calling out, "Trick or treat!" the lady of the house commented on their costume, then teasingly said, "Gee . . . I don't know how to give you your treat. I don't know if you are one, one and a half, or TWO trick-or-treaters! Should I give you one, one and a half, or TWO treats?!" causing the frustrated answer, "Stir it UP, silly!" to come from the delayed trick-or-treating girls!

Three-year-old Boomer was always very uneasy being in the bathroom by himself. Usually, his mother would stay in there with him.

One particular time, however, due to Boomer's mother not being home, his father was in there, sitting on the rim of the bathtub while Boomer was on the toilet.

Then, standing up, Dad said, "I'll be right back, Boomer. I need to go do something, but I will be right back."

He left the bathroom and returned in a very short time. Breathing a sigh of relief, little Boomer said, "I sure am glad that you came back, Daddy! Mommy tells me that SHE will be right back, but she doesn't and it makes me awful IRRIGATED!"

The family was at Grandma's house. Three-year-old Betsy was watching (with big round eyes) as her older brother spread the apple butter on his buttered toast, took a big bite, then licked his lips.

For some reason, she was not sharing the treat with him. She was quietly hanging back . . . just watching.

"Do you want a bite, Betsy?" Jesse offered.

Vehemently shaking her head, "NO!" she answered in a firm tone of voice.

"Why not? It's GOOD!" and he smacked his lips, again.

" 'Cause . . . it's POOP!" an indignant Betsy answered.

Just about every time the family was ready to leave the house going on a trip, Mom would make the statement: "Well . . . let's hit the trail."

One day, after they had been driving for quite a while, three-and-a-half-year-old Brent asked, "Dad, WHEN are we gonna hit the TRAILER?"

Little Mandy had always wanted a baby sister (or baby brother) in the family. When Mom told Mandy that she was going to get a baby sister or brother, Mandy was VERY excited. In fact, she could hardly wait!

Shortly after her infant sister was brought home from the hospital, six-year-old Mandy wanted to spend the night (AND/OR) weekend with just ANYONE, because, "THIS baby cries too MUCH!"

In Collette's first-grade class at school, there was a little Negro girl no one would play with. Six-and-a-half-year-old Collette decided that SHE would go play with her. The two little girls played happily together for the rest of the day.

That evening, Collette was telling her mother and father, "There is a Negro girl in my class that no one will play with, but I played with her and we had lots of fun."

He complimented her, "That's nice, Collette. You know, the longer you play together, the more fun the two of you will have, and it won't be very long and you won't even notice that she is a different color. . . . It will seem like she is a white girl, like you!"

About two days later, Collette informed him, "You were right, Daddy. The palms of her hands are ALREADY turning white!"

After going through her first head-lice check at school, with her first-grade teacher's admonition to the students fresh in her mind, "Be SURE, now, and have your parents look for head lice in YOUR hair . . . " little six-year-old Daisy asked, "Daddy, will you please look in my hair to see if I have any head MICE?"

On a vacation trip down into California, the family was going through the giant redwood forest.

Pointing at different growth rings on the stump of a two-thousand-year-old tree, Jesse's grandmother was explaining, "This was the year they signed the Magna Carta," pointing to another ring, "The year Columbus discovered America," and another ring, "the Declaration of Independence!"

Ten-year-old Jesse didn't seem to be too impressed, however, until his grandmother said, "You know that gate we came through and we walked through that tree stump? Well . . . I brought your daddy through that SAME gate when HE was three years old!"

"WOW! Is it THAT old?!" Jesse wanted to know.

While driving along on the freeway, the family car had just passed a hitchhiker carrying a sign: "WASH," indicating the man wanted a ride to somewhere in the state of Washington.

Nine-and-a-half-year-old Stevie asked her father, "Dad, they won't be having a CAR-WASH out here on the FREEWAY, will they?"

Being small-boned and slender in stature was especially helpful to ten-year-old Harold one particular weekend.

Yes, one weekend, young Harold was called on to climb up on the roof and through a window, to unlock the door of his grandparents' house, also, to climb up on the really slippery metal roof and squeeze through a window to unlock his parents' house; as well as to climb up the steep roof and in through a window to unlock the door of his aunt's apartment!

At school on Monday, young Harold informed his teacher and classmates, "I don't have anything to show, but I certainly have something to tell. . . . I got to be a HERO!"

The sight of seventeen-month-old Alex on his stomach on the floor, squirming about, his arms and legs flailing wildly, caused his sister to ask, "WHAT are you DOING?"

To which baby Alex proudly answered, "I SWIMMIN'!"

In the car, two-and-a-half-year-old Megan had been listening to her parents discussing Grandpa Art's heart surgery while on their way to see him.

Later, coming into his hospital room, little Megan's greeting: "Hi, Grandpa Aht. . . . How's youh HAHT!"

Grandpa worked the night shift and, naturally, slept during the day. He would leave his dentures soaking in the bathroom while he was sleeping.

Grandma would always tell visiting grandchildren, "Don't play with Grandpa's teeth, 'cause they'll BITE you!"

One day, two-and-a-half-year-old Dawn went into the bathroom. Since she was in there longer than she should have been, Grandma decided to check, calling to warn, "Now, don't you play with Grandpa's teeth, 'cause they'll BITE you!" while going into the bathroom.

Little Dawn, with Grandpa's false teeth in her tiny hands, informed her, "No they DON'T, Grandma!"

Two-year-old Tyler was being swung around and around by his father. When he put Tyler back on his feet, little Tyler was VERY dizzy and (naturally) staggered around, claiming, "HEY! The HOUSE is spinning! Quick, Mommy, QUICK! Take me outside so I can see the house spin!"

Seven-year-old Richard's aunt and uncle had just purchased his parents' camper. Due to his aunt's extreme fear of (and respect for) black widow spiders, Richard had been EXPLICITLY instructed how and where to spray that empty camper with the insecticide so as to kill ANY spiders (ESPECIALLY black widows) that might be lurking there.

When he came back into the house, his aunt asked, "Richard, did you do a GOOD job spraying that camper? I want to know . . . did you spray ALL the corners of the shower? IN and ALL around the stool? IN the bathroom cabinet, as well as the washbasin?"

She continued, "Are you SURE you sprayed around the table and ESPECIALLY in the corners of the seats AROUND the table, as well as ALL the corners around the bed? And did you do a good job putting that spray over ALL the carpet? Are you SURE?"

"I sure DID, Aunt Georgia!" he boasted. "You should have seen 'em. . . . Why, all those spiders were just STANDIN' in LINE to get out!"

When seven-year-old Tanya's throat was sort of plugged, she kept trying to clear it. However, it wouldn't stay cleared.

All of her throat clearing caused her dad to nonchalantly explain, "Oh . . . you've just got a frog in your throat."

A short time later, however, she was in the kitchen and her dad heard the sounds of her SPITTING! Going into the kitchen, he asked, "What are you doing, spitting on the floor?"

"I'm trying to spit those FROGS out of my throat!" explained a worried Tanya.

121

Nine-and-a-half-year-old Wimpy's name for Grants Pass, Oregon: "GRASS PANTS, OREGON!"

Four-year-old Jason was watching the Disney Channel on his grandmother's TV set. He was watching Dumbo, the flying elephant.

"They're LYING, Grandma!" Jason said. "Elephants can't fly!"

"They aren't lying, Jason," Grandma explained. "That is a FAIRY tale."

Later that day, Grandma called Jason's house, and Jason answered the telephone. "Hi, Jason. Is your mother there?"

"No, Grandma, my mom's not here. I'm here all alone. I am taking care of everything, all by myself."

In the background, Jason's mother could be heard saying, "You're lying, Jason!"

"Are you lying to me, Jason?" Grandma wanted to know.

"No, I'm not lying, Grandma. That's an ELEPHANT tale!"

Four-year-old Lisa had gone to church and, while there, witnessed several baptisms.

When she came home, her dad asked, "What went on there at church, Lisa? What did you do?"

"OK . . . but they were DROWNING everybody!" was little Lisa's version of what had gone on.

High overhead, a jet plane was leaving its white streamer across the blue sky.

While pointing up at it, four-year-old Phillip cried out, "Look, Mommy! He's painting the sky!"

Looking down at the wrench being used by Great-Grandpa, little four-year-old Elizabeth commented, "THAT looks JUST like my DADDY'S wrench!"

Two-and-a-half-year-old Jacob had just told his grandmother, "God makes mistakes," causing his grandmother to ask, "What mistake has God made, Jacob?"

"He made dandy-lions, Grandma. And my daddy HATES dandy-lions!"

The two very solemn-faced little girls sitting together in church were sisters, one two years old and the other three. They were sitting very straight and still, not speaking, smiling, or even looking around.

Wanting them to relax, a member of the church lovingly put her hand on the arm of one of the girls, but quickly withdrew it when the little girl in a snarling tone of voice said, "Get your COTTON-PICKIN' hand OFFA me!"

Two-year-old Alec had been promised a ride on the Kellogg, Idaho, gondola. He was really looking forward to this and was pretty excited.

The closer they got to Kellogg, the more excited Alec became. By the time they pulled into the parking lot and got their first look at the gondola, little Alec was beside himself with excitement, stating, "M-m-m! I LIKE this, Dad! I want you to buy ME one JUST like it!"

Three-year-old April just loved to look at the moon at night.

One night, while viewing a full moon with her grandmother, a surprised little April exclaimed, "OH! It's not CUT anymore, Grandma!"

Five-year-old Charlie and his mother were working together in the garden when she decided to tell him about the new baby growing in her tummy.

"A new baby? How did it get into YOUR tummy, Mama?" he wanted to know.

"Well, Charlie," she said, "your daddy planted a seed in my tummy and the baby is growing from that seed your daddy planted. Sort of like when we plant a seed in our garden and something grows from that seed."

One day, not too long after the baby was born, the family decided to show her off to Roy. Now, Roy was a bachelor and an old friend of the family. They found Roy out behind his house, working in his own large garden.

While cradling their new baby in his arms, looking down into the infant's sweet face, Roy said, "Hey, now! THIS is just what I need! I think I just might keep her right here, with me!"

Little Charlie, however, decided differently. "YOU got a big garden, Roy. If YOU want a baby, you plant your OWN seed!"

The little five-year-old girl and her father were walking past a brick house just down the road from their own home.

Pointing to the male dog lying on the porch of the brick house the girl's father said, "Look, hon, there is Trevor's puppies' daddy," referring to their own female dog, Trevor.

"Does he ever go see Trevor and the puppies, Daddy?"

"No."

She thought for a few minutes, then asked, "What'd she do . . . DUMP him?"

On the long trip from Wisconsin to North Idaho in his friend's family car, eight-year-old Sean kept letting go with some pretty rotten-smelling stinkers. Everyone in the car was suffering AND complaining.

Thinking that it might (in some way) help him to stop, Joan said, "You know, Sean, I have heard someone say that a person that lets stinkers just COULD have a mental problem!"

A short time later, tapping on Joan's arm, Sean told her confidently, "I think you're right, Joan. . . . I think I just had another mental problem!"

Jane, a riding instructor, had been giving eight-year-old Maris Kay riding lessons. For the first three lessons, Jane (while riding one horse) led Shelly, a big, gentle thoroughbred, around the track with Maris Kay in the saddle.

On the fourth lesson, Jane informed Maris Kay, "This time, I am going to drop the lead rope. You know Shelly, now, and you're not afraid of her . . . right? When you want Shelly to do something, just tell her what you want. That's all there is to it."

A short time later, Maris Kay wanted Shelly to turn (to the left). With her left arm straight out, Maris Kay was telling Shelly, "TURN, Shelly! TURN!"

"M-m-m . . . this chicken sure is good! What are we having tomorrow night?" Eight-year-old Sean wanted to know.

"Liver," Joan answered.

A little later, a piece of chicken was missing from the plate of Joan's daughter. After considerable searching, it couldn't be found, and she was given another piece.

That's right! Young Sean had snitched that piece of chicken off her plate and put it away for himself, so HE wouldn't have to eat liver the following night!

Driving along, Dad was cautioned about loose gravel by a sign stating: "Watch for loose gravel."

Trying to pull a cutie, Dad exclaimed (in an extra loud voice), "OH . . . NO! Loose GRAVEL! I wonder who let all of that GRAVEL loose?!"

Immediately four-year-old Betsy wanted to know, "WHERE, Daddy? WHERE? Oh, yeah . . . NOW, I see it!"

One of Uncle Dick's hands has a missing little finger.

One day, while watching his four-year-old nephew, Rocky, tracing a stick along the cracks in the porch floor, Uncle Dick decided to pull a trick on little Rocky. He put his hand (with the missing finger) down on the board, right in front of the stick, and Rocky drew the stick over Uncle Dick's hand. Uncle Dick jerked his hand back, loudly crying out, "OH! See what YOU did?!"

Immediately little Rocky jumped off the porch and down onto his knees to look under the porch for the missing finger!

Later, amid the laughter, Uncle Dick explained that his finger had been missing for a very long time, to which a sheepish little Rocky confessed, "I WONDERED why there was no blood!"

Being allergic to bee stings, April's grandmother was frantically trying to flip a bumblebee from her apron. She managed to brush it off before it stung her.

April's mother, worrying about her mother, asked, "Are you all right, Mom? Did it STING you?"

To which little four-year-old April added, "Grandma . . . did that bee-bumble git you?"

In some unknown manner, four-year-old Bobby had gotten possession of a paper cup (his LATEST pride and joy).

When his older cousin, Gail, stopped in to visit Bobby and his mother, little Bobby brought Gail a drink of water in "his" paper cup. There was about one inch of water in the cup.

After about the sixth such drink of water, Gail asked, "Where are you getting this water from?"

"From the toilet!" the honest little Bobby explained.

Four-year-old Angie had gotten a little toy dish set for her birthday. She had been serving her older brother, five-year-old Ryan, all kinds of imaginary food . . . sandwiches, pie, crackers and cheese, coffee, etc., etc.

126

"Ryan, would you like another sandwich?" Angie asked.

"No," he answered. "I am just TOO full. I couldn't hold ONE more bite!"

At that moment, their grandmother and great-grandmother came in, saying, "Come on, get your coats and shoes on, and we'll all go down to Bud's Drive-In for a hamburger, french fries, and ice cream!"

To which little Angie replied, "OK. I'll go, but RYAN is too full! HE can't hold one more bite!"

Four-and-a-half-year-old Curtis was being taken to the baby-sitter. On the icy road, the car was slipping and sliding all over.

His mother said the usual little prayer: "Jesus, keep us safe."

Little Curtis asked, "Mommy, is Jesus EVERYWHERE?"

"Yeah . . . yeah, I guess so, Curtis. Why?" she asked.

"Well, if He is EVERYwhere, then He must be in MY stomach . . . 'cause I sure am getting SICK!"

Six-year-old Ricky had been saving up his money to buy Christmas presents for his sisters and brothers. His mother had been giving him five cents for each chore he finished, so he had four dollars and fifty cents (four one-dollar bills and two quarters) accumulated by the time he went to shop. Unknown to little Ricky, Dad had slipped a twenty-dollar bill in with Ricky's four dollars and fifty cents.

At the store, Ricky picked out one present, took it to the cashier, and handed her the twenty-dollar bill. Upon receiving the change, Ricky couldn't believe all the money he was getting back and asked the cashier, "Are you SURE you haven't made a mistake?"

After checking the sales slip, she assured Ricky that everything was right.

Ricky continued buying gifts (going back with each gift and paying the cashier for that gift) until his list was filled.

Later that evening, a very satisfied little Ricky shared the news with his family: "I have finished MY Christmas shopping . . . and I have more money NOW than I had when I started!"

For some reason of her own, Nina had always fiercely defended her little brother. NO . . . no matter WHAT Richard was being accused of, Nina seemed to ALWAYS come up with a way out for him.

One day, their mother was very upset with little two-and-a-half-year-old Richard and angrily asked, "RICHARD! Did you mess your pants again?"

In quick defense of her little brother, six-year-old Nina stated "NO! HE didn't," adding, "It must have been that kid at the park you were playing with. . . . HE did it! Didn't he, Baby?"

During a recent death and subsequent funeral, friends and neighbors had left food at the family home of the bereaved, as well as preparing and serving dinner after the funeral.

Later, while everyone was endeavoring to return the empty dishes back to their rightful owners, a lively discussion was taking place on the front porch of Kyle's grandmother concerning HER dishes. "Is this ALL of yours? Are you SURE, now, that we have everything?" was being asked at the front door, while at the same time five-year-old Kyle was trying to keep Grandma's attention, causing little Kyle to be sent to his bedroom until after Harry (the man at the door) had left.

Going into Kyle's bedroom, Grandma explained, "Kyle, you shouldn't talk to me while Harry was talking. Little kids aren't SUPPOSED to talk at the same time BIG people are talking. It isn't polite!"

"But, Grandma . . . you've got TWO ears, ain't cha?" an innocent little Kyle asked.

Five-year-old Annie was listening to the two older ladies visiting. The remark: "I sure do miss the GOOD OLD DAYS" caused little Annie to ask, "What did it do, get old and die?"

On the way to church on Easter morning, his aunt asked five-year-old Brian if he knew what Easter was all about.

"Yes," Brian answered. "Easter is the day Jesus arose from the tomb and went to Heaven." Then, with a very serious expression on his face, little Brian continued, "But you know . . . I just don't think he'll do that again!"

Five-year-old Christi asked, "Mommy, why does candy make holes in your teeth? So it can get out?"

Three-year-old Thomas was at his grandmother's house. She was trying to clear her throat. With her lips compressed, she was making a growling sound deep in her throat.

Little Thomas was (naturally) concerned and asked, "What are you doing, Grandma?"

"Oh . . . I have a frog in my throat, Thomas. It's nothing," she said.

Which caused Thomas to climb up on her lap and attempt to open her mouth with his little fingers. Then, looking down into her open mouth, he told her, "I don't see no frog, Grandma! Maybe it's SLEEPING!"

While on a trip to New Orleans with her husband, Lois kept looking around for a gift to take home for their three-year old-daughter, Brenda. Everything she thought about buying, Jim would tell her, "You don't want that! In fact, don't buy ANYTHING here."

Lois didn't buy anything for a few days. However, she walked into one store and fell in love with a Negro baby doll in a pink cradle there.

When she showed it to Jim, he told her, "You don't want that, either, 'cause you can't take it home to Idaho on the airplane."

She did, though. She carried it.

Little Brenda opened her present from New Orleans. Seeing the little Negro doll, Brenda wrinkled her nose, asking, "Is dis de only color it cum'd in, Mommy?"

Three-year-old Mike's pronunciation of piano was "PAY-AN-OH," and his four-year-old cousin Rinnie's name for Mike was "MACKO."

"Anyone with any smarts at all knows better than to EAT anything you catch out of THERE!" was the comment concerning fishing in the San Francisco Bay. Adding, "However it is not unusual to see fishermen scattered here and there, fishing from the docks at the edge of the water as you drive along."

Dad was spending the day fishing with his five-and-a-half-year-old son, Jimmy. It was just the two of them, sharing a GOOD day, fishing there in the San Francisco Bay.

When his dad wanted to throw the ugly fish (that Jimmy had caught) back into the water, Jimmy objected. Later, however, after the fish had been cleaned and fried, little Jimmy decided, "I ketched em ALL for you, Dad!"

Five-year-old GayeAnn was going to the movies with Grandma.

Getting closer to movie time (as well as to the theater), GayeAnn worriedly asked, "But, Grandma, where are YOU going to sit?"

"Oh, they have all kinds of seats in there, GayeAnn."

"But YOU can't fit in any of them, Grandma. . . . You're too BIG!"

The family was on a vacation trip. In the backseat of the family car, the two brothers were playing a game:

"What kind of a noise does a horse make?"

Five-and-a-half-year-old Paul whinnied like a horse.

"What kind of a noise does a cow make?"

Paul moooed like a cow.

But when asked, "What kind of a noise does a cougar make?" Paul didn't know and wanted time to think on it. About thirty minutes later, little Paul decided that cougars go, "COO-GRR! COO-GRR!"

———————

Usually, after Bible study each week, it was standard procedure to stop off at Grandma and Grandpa's house for ice cream.

One time, Grandpa was sick and didn't go to Bible study. Later, he heard them come into the house and little four-year-old Mari called out, "Grandpa! Grandpa . . . your little DARLIN'S here!"

———————

Charlie's dad is a logger. Sometimes he has had to stay in logging camps close to his job during the work week, taking his meals there in the camp and going home on weekends.

At one of these logging camps, it was the custom of the cooks to give the men a fresh orange with each meal. Charlie's dad would save all of his oranges and take them home at the end of the week.

While at home one weekend, Dad decided to try to explain his job to four-year-old Charlie. Starting up his chainsaw, Dad cut down a bush in the yard. "See, Charlie . . . THAT'S how I make a living . . . cutting down the trees. Now . . . YOU tell ME how Daddy makes money?"

To which little Charlie quickly answered, "Daddy cuts down da trees and picks up da ORANGES!"

———————

In the car on the way to Spokane, four-and-a-half-year-old Tanya and her six-year-old sister, Jennifer, were arguing about Tanya's ability to read. Jennifer saying, "YOU can't read. . . .

YOU don't know HOW!" and Tanya arguing, "I do TOO know how to read!" back and forth . . . back and forth.

Finally, Jennifer thrust a small slip of paper to Tanya, instructing, "Here! Read THIS!"

Tossing her head, little Tanya instantly answered, "I don't WANT to!"

Author's note: I have a little game I play with little children when they are visiting with us. It goes like this: I tell them, "When you ask for something, the magic word is *please* . . . right? Now, that is at everyone ELSE'S house. Our children are all grown-up and have left home. Our two dogs always tell us, WOOF WOOF, when they want something . . . so, the magic word HERE is *WOOF WOOF!*" I will then offer them candy or a cookie IF they tell me, "WOOF WOOF."

Three-year-old Douglas had just been told, "Although the magic word is *please* for everyone ELSE, you have to tell ME 'WOOF WOOF.' " I then offered him some jelly beans.

He wanted the jelly beans, telling me, "Please."

"No, Douglas," I said, "you have to tell ME, 'WOOF WOOF.' "

He didn't seem to want to do that, so I pretended to start to put the candy back into the sack, causing the instant reply of: "ARF! ARF!"

Over the telephone, the tearful three-year-old Katy was telling her grandmother about her new glass (plastic) slippers.

"Oh, Grandma," little Katy wailed, "Peppy just RUINED my glass slipper!"

"Now, Katy, HOW did Peppy ruin your glass slipper?"

"He POO-POOED on it!"

"LOOK! Look at my hands, Grandma. See how HAPPY my hands are!"

Grandma looked at, and commented on, her little grandson's "happy" hands.

Then, expecting a nice remark about the many things she had done, Grandma spread her own hands and asked, "What do MY hands tell YOU?"

"That you're an old TATTLETALE!"

Seven-year-old Christy was staying with some friends. Four cans of Coke were being kept cold in the refrigerator for the four girls. Christy asked, and was given permission, to drink her Coke before the other girls wanted theirs.

Later, Christy asked for another Coke.

"No, Christy. You've already had yours and there is only enough for the other girls," their mother explained.

"Well, could I please have one of THEIR Cokes, then?" Christy wanted to know.

The answer, again, was: "No."

Puckering up and turning on the tears, Christy complained, "Well, I can't help it if my mom got me hooked on Cokes!"

While sucking on a piece of licorice, Bobby dropped it on the floor.

"You go wash that off, Bobby!" his mother ordered.

"Why?" Bobby wanted to know. "It's ALREADY black!"

Eight-year-old Christi was visiting her grandma and grandpa in Idaho. Grandpa was showing Christi "all my fine-feathered friends" (Idaho's wild birds, i.e., grouse, etc., etc.).

After a few days, Christi asked, "Grandpa, why are you SHOOTING your feathered FRIENDS?"

When seven-year-old Michael was asked, "Hey . . . where

did you get those cute dimples?" he calmly explained, "I fell into the corner of our garage. THAT'S how I got them!"

———————

Jennifer's mother was getting worried. You see . . . just about EVERYTHING had been tried, and so far, NOTHING had worked to get five-year-old Jennifer to stop the bad habit she had of sucking her thumb . . . and Jennifer would start to kindergarten the coming September!

As a last resort, Jennifer's mother decided to have a talk with her concerning this bad habit. "Jennifer, do you know that you have a bad habit?"

"What's a habit?" Jennifer wanted to know.

Her mother explained, "A habit is something you do and you don't even know you are doing it . . . like sucking your thumb! Now, you don't want to be sucking your thumb when you start to kindergarten, do you?"

"NO!" Jennifer exclaimed, while putting her thumb in her mouth.

Her mother reached over and gently pulled the little hand down. "See what I mean?"

Then, after much discussion between the two, they came up with a plan to help Jennifer break her habit. Every time Jennifer's thumb was seen in her mouth, the code expression *cherry cheesecake!* (Jennifer's choice of words) was spoken, and Jennifer's thumb would instantly come out of her mouth!

When she started kindergarten, little Jennifer's bad habit had been broken . . . thanks to ALL of that cherry cheesecake!

———————

On a trip to his mother's homeland, young Phillip and his mother were in his uncle's car, going to his uncle's house in West Germany. It was dusk and the moon was shining over the countryside.

Phillip looked out the car window, then tugged frantically at his mother's sleeve, exclaiming, "MOM! Mom, LOOK! They've even got a moon in GERMANY!"

Company at the dinner table and four-year-old Delmer's mother had made some oyster stew. When Delmer took his first spoonful of the stew, he had this to say: "Mom . . . I hate to tell you this . . . but I think you got some DIRT in your stew!"

A little boy, about four years old, came into the Spokane (Washington) Airport with his parents.

While his parents were still in the security check-in line, the little fella broke away and darted into the exit lane.

His mother was frantically calling his name, telling him, "You can't GO that way! You come back here with us!"

The little guy ran up one side of the two concourse ramps, around the saddle (at the top), then back down the other ramp, after which he stopped and gave his mother the "SEE! I CAN *TOO* DO IT" look.

After stubbing his toe, four-year-old Cody went into the house, tearfully telling his mother, "I hurt my MAMA toe!"

The two sisters, six-year-old Cami and four-year-old Mari, were doing riding tricks on their bicycles, showing off for their grandparents.

Cami stopped riding and was watching and laughing at Mari's tricks, causing little Mari to complain, "Don't be GREEDY, Cami! I didn't laugh at YOU when you did your tricks!"

Six-year-old Georgia was in the first grade. Due to the low grades on Georgia's report card, her mother was upset and angry. Mom wanted Georgia to DO her schoolwork AND turn it in on time, so her grades would come up.

Comparing her low grades with the grades of her sister (a

third-grader), Georgia's mother scolded, "Why don't YOU get some of those A's like Jeanette does?"

Back at school, little Georgia went to Jeanette's teacher, requesting, "Will you please give MY teacher some of your A's? 'Cause my mom wants ME to have some of those A's like Jeanette got!"

Six-year-old Jill was sharing her sparkly stickers with the other children in her first-grade classroom.

When Jill got home from school later that afternoon, she was crying pretty hard. Her mother wanted to know what Jill's problem was.

The heartbroken Jill informed her mother that SHE didn't have any sparkly stickers left . . . that she had given ALL of them away!

"Why didn't you keep one for yourself, honey?" Mom asked.

"Oh, I couldn't have done THAT, Mommy! Why . . . if I had kept one for ME, then THELMA wouldn't have had one!"

It was 12:15 P.M. Mom and five-year-old Ricky were walking along a busy street in Fircrest/Tacoma, Washington. Conditions were quiet one minute, and the next minute pandemonium broke loose directly across the street from them!

With jellied knees, the dumbfounded mother watched with her young son as five city police cars, one sheriff's car, and two taxicabs (one with an open door) converged on the scene! Four young policemen, two of them swinging their sticks (like the sticks used on Rodney King), were chasing a big Negro man. They caught him and wrestled him to the ground while a voice was heard ordering, "Don't hit him! Don't hit him. . . . it's not worth it!"

After the big man had been restrained and was on the way to the police car, little Ricky sang out in a very loud and clear voice the theme song of *Cops!*

Five-year-old Joshua didn't like to have to untie his shoes before putting them on. He (naturally) had a lot of trouble putting/getting them on, with lots of crying and stress.

One day, his mother was watching as he was going through the battle of putting on his tied shoes. "Joshua," she said, "if you would only untie your shoes BEFORE you try to put them on, you would find out they would go on MUCH easier!"

Nothing doing! So . . . after much effort, frustration, anger, and tears from Joshua, his mother commented, "Well . . . it is not unusual for a person to have one foot maybe one half-inch longer than their other foot or even one hand a little bigger than their other hand!"

Little Joshua wanted to know, "WHY?!"

"I don't know, hon," his mother said.

Thinking about it for a short time, Joshua decided, "I'll bet I know! I'll bet God ran out of DIRT!"

––––––––––

Jimmy's family was getting ready to go on a vacation trip. The plane was to meet Dad at the plant after his shift and leave from there. Jimmy's mother and his three older sisters had been working hard at putting everything in the car, and they were all ready to go . . . but they couldn't find the car keys!

Knee-high to a grasshopper, little Jimmy had playfully decided to hide the car keys! After more than an hour of looking all over (with no luck), his sister Janice (with whom he always traded secrets) talked him into sharing his secret of where he had hidden them.

Janice then ran into the house, screaming, "I found them! I found them!"

A scowling Jimmy informed his sister, "I'm not EVER gonna tell YOU nuthin' again, Janice!"

––––––––––

Four-year-old GayeAnn was wanting her grandmother to drive faster and faster.

"I can't do THAT; the cops will pick me up!" Grandma said.

"Oh, they can't pick YOU up, Grandma. . . . You're too heavy!" GayeAnn reasoned.

It was Grandpa's birthday! On the way over to Grandpa's house, four-year-old Bobby was warned by his parents, "Now, Bobby, don't you tell Grandpa what he has in his package."

"I won't," Bobby assured them.

While getting out of the car in Grandpa's driveway, Bobby was, again, reminded, "Now remember, Bobby, don't you tell Grandpa what's in his package."

"No," Bobby agreed.

Carrying Grandpa's present into the house, Bobby said, "Hi, Grandpa. Here is your blue shirt we brought you!"

Her first job as a carhop, and a very scared fifteen-year-old Dolly was trying to impress others around her by playing it "cool."

She had placed a pencil over her ear (as she had seen other carhops do) and, with the order pad in hand, started walking toward the car. Her FIRST customer!

Young Dolly's heart was pounding! The closer to the car she got, the more scared she became, and right at the last moment, she started running!

Yep . . . ran right off (with her boss's order pad and pencil) and didn't go back!

Twelve-year-old Mark was a city boy from California, used to getting all of their food from a grocery store. When the family moved to Montana, it became one of Mark's duties to purchase eggs from the farmer down the road.

On one such occasion, upon Mark's return, his mother asked, "Where did you put the eggs, Mark?"

"They didn't have any, Mom," Mark answered. "I asked why, and they told me the hens were melting!"

Realizing that Mark had misunderstood, that he had really

meant "MOLTING," his mother teasingly asked, "MELTING? Now, Mark, HOW could those hens be MELTING!"

To which young Mark quickly answered, "Darned if I know! It's when they start losing their feathers and quit laying eggs. . . . You know . . . MELTING!"

The third-grader had left his composition book at home. Realizing this, he asked, "May I go home?"

"Why, Robert?" his teacher wanted to know.

" 'Cause I left my CONSTIPATION book at home," Bob explained.

Due to extra-harsh economic conditions, three-year-old Bonnie lived with another family while her mother worked elsewhere. Every chance she could get, Mom would visit with her little daughter.

One day, coming into the small café where Bonnie and the lady she was staying with were having ice cream, Mom gave little Bonnie a big hug, asking, "How's Mama's little girl today?"

Looking up at the waitress, little Bonnie bragged, "I have POO [two] mommies!"

At church, three-year-old Jacob was listening to the pastor's sermon about Jesus, Son of God.

Leaning over, little Jacob whispered, "OOPS! He [the minister] said a bad word, Daddy!"

Later, while shaking hands at the door, Jacob accused the minister, "YOU said a bad word!"

"Oh? I said a bad word? Just WHAT was it I said, Jacob?" the pastor wanted to know.

"You said, 'Son of . . . ' " Then, covering his mouth, little Jacob quickly turned his face into his father's pant leg.

Three-year-old Ivy had been requesting to spend some time at her aunt's house. Finally, given permission, little Ivy was spending Sunday afternoon with her aunt.

After spending only a couple of hours there, little Ivy informed her aunt, "I have to go to my REAL home . . . and to my REAL family!"

At the zoo, five-year-old Ricky had gotten pecked by a turkey.

Helping their busy mother out, his older sister, Eli, took the crying Ricky into their motor home.

In a short time, Mom was able to go to the motorhome also. Expecting to see a VERY upset, tearful Ricky, Mom was VERY surprised to see Ricky sitting next to Eli, laughing and talking with his sister!

Mom asked the thirteen-and-a-half-year-old Eli, "How did you get Ricky calmed down so QUICK?"

Eli explained, "It was EASY! I just told him not to worry; we'll get even with THAT old turkey when Thanksgiving gets here!"

Little Ricky added, "Yeah! We'll get even then! We'll have TURKEY for Thanksgiving DINNER!" Then he gave a devious, "HEH! HEH! HEH!"

Six-year-old Annie was sitting on the lap of a dear family friend she liked to call Aunt Georgia, listening to the discussion between Aunt Georgia and Annie's mother about children, grandchildren, and great-grandchildren, as Aunt Georgia had just finished telling about her granddaughter being pregnant with her second baby.

"It doesn't seem like I should be OLD enough to have GREAT-grandchildren yet!" Aunt Georgia lamented.

At this time, Annie's mother offered, "Do you want another piece of cake, Georgia?"

"No," Georgia answered, adding, "It's good, but I'm too fat now."

Little Annie intervened, "I don't think Aunt Georgia is too fat! Do YOU, Mama? I think she's too GREAT-GRANDMA!"

Grandpa had picked Danny up from kindergarten. When they got home, he gave Danny six small pieces of Hershey's candy.

Danny places one piece down on the arm of Grandpa's chair, claiming, "THIS one's for ME." Placing another piece alongside the first piece, he said, "And this one's for Crystal," then (in turn), "This one's for me and this one's for Crystal. This one's for me and this one's for Crystal."

Looking at the double row of candy for about half a minute, Danny put a piece of "HIS" candy in his mouth and picked up a piece of "CRYSTAL'S" candy and put it in his mouth.

Again, he put another piece of "HIS" candy in his mouth, then another piece of "CRYSTAL'S."

After putting the last piece of "HIS" candy in his mouth, little Danny cocked his head slightly to one side for just a second or two before stating, "As fast as this candy goes, it's hardly worth saving ONE piece for Crystal!" He THEN popped that last piece into his mouth!

Mom, Dad, and their seven children were finishing a two-and-a-half-week vacation trip in their motor home.

Tired, cramped, and sometimes pretty cranky, the children had started blaming their dad for just about everything before they got back home. (Gee . . . he WAS the DRIVER!) In fact, it had gotten to the point where someone would start out, "Dad . . . " and Dad would interrupt, "Don't call ME Dad. . . . MY name is MUD!"

The day after returning home, Dad and five-year-old Ricky went into the Bureau of Vital Statistics.

Walking into the office, little Ricky told the two men behind the counter, "HI! My name is Ricky, and this is m-m-m-m . . . and . . . and this guy here . . . HIS name is MUD!"

If something was being said by his parents (or ANYONE, for that matter) that this little three-year-old Mullan, Idaho, resident didn't want to hear, little Jack's instant comeback: "DOAN TALKKA ME!" was always there!

Three-year-old Alex was tugging at his father's belt. "Me want gum, Daddy! Me want gum!"

Dad was visiting with someone and ignoring little Alex, who was still insisting, "Me want GUM, Daddy!"

Not getting his dad's attention, Alex decided to try his mother. In a whining voice, he said, "Me want GUM, Mommy!"

Breaking into her husband's conversation, she asked (in an exasperated tone of voice), "Why don't you take Alex for a walk and get him some gum?"

"No . . . I need to take the car down to the gas station later. I'll get him some gum then."

Quickly changing his mind, Alex informed his father, "NO! I just want a CANDY BAR!"

Grandpa liked to take Jesse with him in the pickup and let Jesse pretend to be driving.

One such day, as three-year-old Jesse was standing on the seat of the pickup (pretending that he was driving), he was moving the gearshift lever, as well as pushing all the different buttons on the dash he could reach.

Little Jesse was reaching to push the cigarette-lighter button in when Grandpa stopped him. "No, Jesse, you can't touch THAT!"

"Why NOT, Grandpa?"

"Because it's got JUICE in it, Jesse."

"Orange juice or apple juice, Grandpa?!"

Since four-year-old Delmer was always running off, at the

142

logging camp, his mother admonished, "Now, Delmer, don't you go up on that hill, 'cause there are bears up there!" She then went back into the cabin.

Looking out the window a short time later, little Delmer was seen running up the logging road just as fast as he could run! His mother ran after him but couldn't quite catch him.

At the top of the hill, his mother looked right and left, but . . . no Delmer. Then, stepping from behind a tree, little Delmer told his mother, "Gee Mom . . . you sure are a funny-looking BEAR!"

Annie had just told her four-year-old cousin, "My mama can't talk, Jason. The doctor took her tonsils out."

Shaking his head slightly, the little fellow wanted to know, "When is he gonna put them back in, so she can talk?!"

Four-year-old Todd was at his grandmother's house. Being busy in the kithen, however, Grandma wasn't paying much attention to him.

The unhappy little fellow was sitting at the kitchen table with a pencil and paper, writing a letter. "Grandma, how do you spell *ick?*"

She raised her eyebrows in surprise. "*I-c-k*, Todd." Then she watched him scribble across the paper.

"How do you spell *or?*" he wanted to know.

"O-r."

Breaking out in sobs as he scribbled his version of *or* on the paper, little Todd explained, "This is what you are doing, Grandma . . . ICKOR [ignoring] me!"

Three-year-old Zack and his mother were having lunch with a friend.

In the café, little Zack was giving his plate of food a doubtful look. Pointing a finger, he asked, "What's THAT, Mommy?"

"Mashed potatoes," she answered.

"Well . . . what's THAT?" Zack asked, pointing to the cauliflower.

"And THAT is cauliflower, Zack. Take a bite. . . . It is mmm-mmm GOOD!"

Evidently, however, he still hadn't been sold on the cauliflower. (He was still giving it a doubting look.) Then, deciding which he wanted to eat, he wanted to share his decision with everyone in the café. Standing up in his booster chair, he aimed and hit the mashed potatoes with the palm of his hand, calling out in a VERY loud voice, "SQUASHED POTATOES!"

The little three-year-old was used to seeing nylon pantyhose. However, upon the first viewing of her aunt's knee-high nylons, little Ivy declared, "THESE are BROKE!"

In trying to prolong the beauty of the Christmas season, Tony's parents had their Christmas tree up and decorated before the middle of December. Why, they had even put some wrapped presents under the tree, with strict instructions to their little three-year-old son, "Now, Tony, don't you dare TOUCH those presents! They are to be opened on Christmas Day."

They later found that little Tony had a hard time waiting for Christmas to get here, because about every five hours he asked, "Is CHRISTMAS here yet?"

The parents of their single-parent daughter had just finishing paying a $3,000 dentist bill for her and her three children.

One day, she stopped in for a surprise visit with her folks. Her eight-year-old son was with her.

Walking into the living room, he said, "Hi, Grandpa!"

Grandpa responded warmly, "Hi there, Daniel. How are you doing today?"

"I'm just a poor boy, Grandpa! BOY . . . you and Grandma are RICH! Why, if you and Grandma weren't spending all this money on all of our teeth, why, YOU would have a MILLION dollars!" was his VERY surprising answer!

Author's note: Many years ago, Shoshone County, Idaho, was dotted with many stills. Consequently, moonshine cabins were prevalent in the area.

One day, at one such moonshine cabin, up the Little River (of the North Fork of the Coeur D'Alene River), about five boys were in the yard playing with dynamite caps.

One of the boys, young Ralph, watched as a big car drove up into the yard. A man got out and went into the cabin.

Coming out later and going to his car, the man stumbled, almost dropping the jug he was carrying.

Ralph asked, "I wonder what's wrong with HIM?"

"Aw-w . . . he's got a SLIVER in his foot," was the nonchalant answer he received.

In the summertime, the small pond down the road was a drawing card to the youngsters in the neighborhood, used for swimming, fishing, etc., etc.

One day, on his trip to the pond, ten-year-old Gene saw a dead cat (all covered with maggots) lying along the road.

Later, at home, he told his family of seeing the dead cat, "All covered with ravies [rabies]!"

The two children were watching as the chimpanzees performed their bicycle-riding skills and tricks on the television screen.

As one of the chimpanzees balanced himself standing on the seat of the moving bicycle, four-and-a-half-year old John (obviously awestruck) declared, "GOSH . . . I can't even do THAT!"

"Well, maybe the chimpanzee is OLDER than you are, John!" six-year-old Linda comforted him.

For about the first three weeks of school, Benjamin's mother couldn't figure out why her six-year-old son was SO ravenous at the end of each school day. Mom made identical lunches for Ben and his older sister and brother, and they weren't NEARLY as hungry as Ben when THEY got home from school. *SO*, she wondered, *What's wrong with Ben?*

The problem had started the first day of school, when one little boy in the group of four Ben was sitting with at lunchtime asked for something Ben had in his lunch bucket. Being a very freehearted little boy, Benjamin gave a quick approval.

Taking a bite the little guy said, "BOY! THAT'S GOOD!"

Then, before long, each of the boys (in turn) asked and was given permission from the freehearted Ben to take something from Ben's lunch bucket.

It soon got to the point where the boys were not asking Ben; they would simply help themselves, leaving poor little Ben with very little (if ANYTHING) to eat!

Needless to say, Benjamin was always REALLY hungry when he got home from school!

According to six-year-old Joni:

"Mary, Mary, quite contrary
How does your garden grow?
With silver bells and TACO shells . . . "

In the café, four-year-old Liam (Irish for William) was acting up. His dad took him into the men's room for a spanking.

Back at their table, Liam was still unhappy and showing it, causing his two-year-old brother, Connor, to ask, "Are you having troubles, Brudder?"

Two-and-a-half-year-old Jamie hadn't been talking very long when at a family picnic (with hamburgers, potato salad, coleslaw, etc., etc., on the menu) she was given some coleslaw (which she had never tasted before) and told, "This is coleslaw, Jamie. Taste it. . . . It's GOOD."

Slowly at first, little Jamie started to eat. After a short time, she decided (out loud), "Oh BOY! Cole-SLOP!"

Two-year-old John's head was covered with curly (very tight curls) blond hair.

Coming into their house one day, his aunt asked, "My GOSH, Johnny . . . where did ALL that curly hair come from?"

"It came with my head!" little Johnny informed her.

Three-year-old Betsy had been enrolled in a speech therapy class for preschoolers. It was her first day of school and little Betsy was pretty excited as the small bright-colored special school bus drove up to the curb where she was waiting.

With her little hands on her tiny hips, little Betsy said (with a lot of expression), "I've been waiting for THIS day all of my LIFE!"

For both roll-your-own-cigarette smokers and the tobacco-chewing residents of Kentucky, the slang word for tobacco is 'backer.

Neither of the two Kentucky residents eighteen-year-old Cousin Sammy or Uncle Mose smoked cigarettes. Both of them, however, chewed tobacco ('backer).

They were working together one day, cleaning out some bottomland, and had a load of logs on a wagon pulled by a team of horses.

Sammy was on the wagon driving the team and Uncle Mose walking beside it when the wagon stopped in the soft, muddy terrain.

With the wagon wheel on his foot, Uncle Mose yelled up to Sammy, "BACK 'ER, SAMMY! Back 'ER!!"

Over his shoulder, Sammy answered, "Sorry . . . I don't have any!"

Being very concerned about the rash on her tiny baby's face, the young mother asked, "What IS it, Grandma? What's causing it?"

After looking at it, Grandma told her not to worry. "Call your doctor and tell him that your Grandma Georgia says the baby has impetigo and would he call in a prescription. . . . Then, we'll go down to the drugstore and pick it up," was Grandma's advice.

She used Grandma's telephone. "Hello, Doctor?" Then, she said, after identifying herself, "Grandma Georgia says to tell you that my baby has BABY-TIGO, and would you call in a prescription for it. . . . We'll go down and pick it up."

February 1, 1993, the first-grade teacher shared with her students the news. "Children," she said, "tomorrow is Ground Hog Day!"

With a suspicious look on his face, one little boy informed her, "Ground HOG'S day?! Well . . . I'M gonna bring a SACK lunch!"

Six-year-old Rhonda and four-year-old Norris were playing Yahtzee together.

Having most of her card full (only the yahtzee was left to be filled), Rhonda picked up the dice and began to shake them.

Norris put his hands together (as if in prayer).

Rhonda immediately stopped shaking the dice, telling Norris, "THAT'S not FAIR! It's not fair to ask God not to let me get my yahtzee!"

"Well . . . maybe I was praying FOR you," little Norris argued.

"Oh . . . THAT'S OK, then!" little Rhonda decided.

Six-year-old Monica and her neighbors, seven-year-old Alex

and his brother, five-year-old Eric, were all playing softball when they accidentally broke a window.

They didn't want to get into trouble and they were all scared. . . . WHAT to do?!

Little Monica determined, "The ONLY thing to do is to go PRAY!"

Walking into her bedroom a short time later, Monica's father found all three of the children on their knees around her bed . . . praying! He decided he needed to look no further for WHO broke the window!

Four-and-a-half-year-old Larry just LOVED hamburgers and french fries. It seemed that no matter WHERE they went to eat, Larry would ALWAYS want a hamburger and french fries.

One time, the family was at a very nice restaurant. The order was placed for steak dinners for the grown-ups, and knowing Larry's love of hamburgers and french fries, his mother (without asking him) ordered for him, "And Larry will have a hamburger and french fries."

To which little Larry complained (in a VERY loud voice), "Why is it THAT'S all I EVER get to eat . . . HAMBURGERS and FRENCH FRIES?!"

Four-year-old Sarah fell in love, at first sight, with the miniature china cup and saucer and tiny matching china pot (on legs) placed on her grandmother's table. Excitedly Sarah exclaimed, over and over, "Ohh . . . how PRETTY, Grandma! Aren't they pretty, Grandma? Can we have a TEA party, Grandma? Aren't they PRETTY!" On and on . . .

Although Grandma tried to explain that they were not supposed to be used for a tea party, little Sarah simply would not be quiet until Grandma gave her some orange juice to drink from the tiny cup!

The four-year-old twins were having lunch at Grandma and Grandpa's house.

"M-m-m . . . these beans sure are good," little Richard complimented. "What kind are they?"

To which his sister, Elizabeth, instantly answered, "PORKEN!"

The home-safety instructions being given to ten-year-old Adam on what he should do when he was home alone: "What to do when we're gone . . . when someone comes to the door, or calls . . . " prompted young Adam to blurt out, "But that's LYING, Mom!"

Fifteen-year-old Gene went up to the county dump with his mother. Expecting some help from her young son, Mom started unloading the load. . . .

Gene had to spit . . . and spit . . . and spit . . . and spit. . . .

"Hey! What is wrong with you?" Mom wanted to know. "What's with all this SPITTING?"

"Well, I don't want any of that dirt and germs getting in ME!" Gene declared.

In the car coming home from the hospital after having visited their mother and new baby sister, Annie, the children were picking on ten-year-old Benjamin.

"Oh, Ben," Elli said in mock disgust, "when they passed out BRAINS . . . you were standing at the end of the line!"

Dad intervened, "ELLI! Now, THAT'S not a very nice thing to say to your brother!"

"That's OK, Dad," Benjamin said calmly, adding, "I guess I WAS standing at the end of the line . . . But THAT just makes MY brain NEWER!"

The family was discussing the candidates before the 1992 election.

Four-year-old Jamie decided, "I like CLINTON, 'cause his HAIR is cool!"

Looking at his fat uncle's round face and big tummy, four-year-old Norris asked, "Uncle Bob, how come your skin is so . . . uh . . . CROWDED?!"

"Grandpa, are you the boss?" four-year-old Jamie asked.
"Yes, I am."
She gave both Grandma and Grandpa an inquisitive look; then, tilting her head slightly, little Jamie declared, "NO, you're NOT, Grandpa!

Mom and Dad had spent the evening (and into the night) playing pinochle with friends, consequently going to bed late.

While they were discussing the preceding evening the following morning, the remark: "I didn't think those folks would EVER go home," was made.

To which little four-year-old Rhonda gave the belated advice: "Why didn't you tell them, 'I guess I'll go to bed, so you folks can go home'?!"

His uncle having darker skin caused four-and-a-half-year-old Matthew to ask, "Aunt Becky, why is Uncle Al black? Is it because Uncle Al used to smoke, so God turned him black?"

Baby Annie had caught a bit of a cold. As she started to whimper, four-year-old Betsy went over to her and, while patting her gently, said, "You are a little princess, Annie! You won't be for very long, but right now, you are our little princess. I think we should call you Little Princess!"

A short time later, while watching his baby sister struggling to breathe through her tiny nose, six-year-old Ricky exclaimed, "MOM! Sister Annie is SNORTING! She may be a princess . . . but she SNORTS!" He then declared, "I think we should call her Princess SNORTS!"

Six-year-old Melanee REALLY loved Coca-Cola. In order to keep her from wanting to drink so MUCH of it, Melanee's mother told her, "No, Melanee, you can't have any more Coke . . . because Coke eats your LIVER!"

Looking down into the empty pop can in front of her, the perplexed Melanee asked, "How can Coke EAT my LIVER? Coke don't even have any TEETH!"

Dad and Mom had asked Grandma to come stay and baby-sit for the week they would be gone. Their home was a VERY busy household, and by the end of the week Grandma was worn out and had caught a bad cold as well. Simply put, she wasn't feeling a bit good . . . and EVERYONE knew it.

Everyone was waiting in the car for Dad to take the family to breakfast at McDonald's when the very concerned six-year-old Ricky ran back into Grandma's bedroom for a last-minute check on her health AND with the plea: "Grandma, PLEASE don't die in OUR house!"

Three-year-old Katie was sitting on her grandfather's lap. Through his half-opened shirt, little Katie spotted the hair on his chest and asked, "Grandpa, where did you get all that hair from?"

Shrugging his shoulders, Grandpa answered, "It's just there."

Sliding down from Grandpa's lap, Katie went to stand in

front of Grandma Betts and asked, "Do YOU have hair on YOUR chest, too?"

"No, I don't."

Then, in a taunting, childish voice, little Katie declared, "Well . . . I don't!"

Great-Grandma's house was one of Jason and Tony's favorite places. They loved to spend time there. However, Grandma hadn't been feeling so good lately, and the only way she would give four-year-old Jason and three-year-old Tony permission to come was: "If you will spend most of the time up the street playing with Matt . . . and DON'T pester me!"

They came, and Jason went up the street to his four-year-old buddy Matt's house.

A short time later, little Tony warned, "Here they come, Grandma . . . to FESTER you up!"

Three-year-old Matt had a cold and (naturally) a runny nose. With the constant wiping, his nose had become very tender, so Mom decided to give him something for his cold.

Handing him a children's decongestant, an orange-flavored chewable tablet, she said, "Here . . . take this, Matt. It's for your cold. Maybe it'll help your nose."

Little Matt took the tablet and put it right up into one nostril of his nose!

For some reason unknown to Mom, a friend of the family who worked at a paper manufacturing mill had given them several big cardboard boxes of dots that came from punching out notebook-paper holes.

When the family moved into a different house, one with a basement, Mom had kept busy cleaning (in turn) each of the main floor rooms but hadn't gotten to the basement (with all of its spiderwebs) yet.

Seven-year-old Sarah and her eight-year-old brother, Jay,

became bored one rainy day. Then they thought of something exciting to do. . . .

Down in the basement, they got into those boxes of dots. By throwing the dots up into the air, they created their own version of snow, so they showered each other with the small white dots.

Later, when Mom went down into the basement to wash some dirty laundry, there were paper dots EVERYWHERE! All over the floor, the washer and dryer, and the Deepfreeze! In the children's hair as well as up on the top of the hooded hanging light! Why, there were even paper dots (resembling stars) caught up in the spiderwebs next to the ceiling and in the corners!

Ah-h, yes! Jay and Sarah had one FUN rainy day!

———————————

The second-grade art class was getting pretty antsy, and when (just before the end of the school day) the room mother made the comment: "It's not over till the fat lady sings," this caused one little boy to look up at his very heavy-set art teacher and ask, "Are YOU going to sing a song?"

———————————

Instead of stating her age as "almost seven," when asked Myra's surprising answer was, proudly: "I am six eleven-twelfths!"

———————————

The little four-year-old knew his great-grandpa was longing to go fishing but didn't have the time to go dig any fishing worms, so Jason, together with his younger cousin, three-year-old Tony, set about surprising their grandpa with a two-pound MJB coffee can almost full of worms . . . earthworms and night crawlers.

Great-Grandpa was thrilled and come Sunday, while he was in his boat out on the lake happily fishing, Jason, his cousin, Tony, and their great-grandma were in a small café in Saint Maries, Idaho, enjoying hamburgers, fries, and milk shakes.

An older lady in an adjoining booth was listening to little Jason and Tony telling about "getting ALL those worms for Grandpa."

Evidently impressed with their story, she commented, "If I had some worms, I'd go fishing, too."

So . . . little Jason pulled two big night crawlers out of his shirt pocket and laid them neatly on the lady's plate, "So SHE can go fishing, too!"

Aaron's grandmother lived next door to a logger who owned and drove his bright red logging truck.

While at Grandma's house one day, little Aaron noticed the logger out there, working on his logging truck. Going next door, Aaron asked, "Harry, can I see inside your truck?"

"You sure can," Harry answered, offering, "Here . . . I'll help you up and you can blow the horn!"

But . . . just as soon as Aaron could see inside the cab, with all the dried mud on the floor and dust on the dash, he wrinkled his nose, telling Harry, "Ooohh . . . you sure do have a DIRTY truck, Harry! Why don't you CLEAN it?"

About a year later, Aaron (now five years old) stopped in for a visit and told Harry's wife, "Gee, you sure have a dirty floor, Mary! Why don't you WASH it?"

From California, little Stephanie (almost three years old) was talking on the phone to her great-grandmother who lived in north Idaho.

"I like you, Grandma," came from the shy little girl.

"I LOVE you, Stephanie!" Great-Grandma answered warmly.

"I love YOU, too, Grandma!"

"Can I come see you, Stephanie?" Great-Grandma asked.

SILENCE! Dead silence.

Then, in the background, Stephanie's grandmother was overheard stating (in a low voice), "You have to TELL her yes, Stephanie! 'Cause Great-Grandma can't SEE you nodding your head over the telephone!"

Two-and-a-half-year-old Brooke was in the living room with her father, watching the news on TV. President Clinton had just made a statement concerning "raising taxes" that caused her dad to groan and make some pretty strong statements against more taxes.

Picking up the telephone, little Brooke called out in a loud, clear voice, "Hello, President Clinton? Bill, don't you raise my daddy's taxes! He don't like that!" She then slammed the telephone receiver down . . . evidently not quite getting it straight, as she picked it back up and, hearing the operator stating, " . . . we cannot put this call through . . . " little Brooke demanded, "WHAT?!" then REALLY slammed the phone back on the hook!

———————

The ornery goose was chasing little Evelyn around the barnyard. Looking back over her shoulder as she ran, little Evelyn warned, "My mama's gonna make SOUP outta you!"

———————

About Robert's father (who suffered from multiple sclerosis) a kindergarten buddy asked, "Is THAT your dad?"

"Yes," Robert answered proudly. "THAT'S MY DAD!"

"What's wrong with him?"

"He has MULTI-PLU-OR-IS-SIS!" five-year-old Robert explained.

———————

In their small north Idaho community it was an established fact that Matt's mother used to have parties and, indeed, drank some herself. She was probably criticized by some of the neighbors, who included the family of a local minister.

When Matt was four years old, the car that his mother was driving (with both Matt and his brother passengers) was hit by a new pickup truck driven by a young intoxicated driver driving at high speed. Matt and his brother were hosptalized and their mother was killed.

For a year, little Matt didn't say much about the accident and didn't talk about his mother, either.

One day, while sitting on a neighbor's porch together with six-year-old Caylan (the minister's son) eating cookies, little five-year-old Matt shared the news, "My mom's an angel, now," causing little Caylan to remark, "WOW! I wonder how she likes the change!"

Debra had planned to spend the day with her five-year-old son, Paul, and his seven-year-old cousin, Jeremiah, at the amusement park.

Listening to his Aunt Debra complaining that an hour had gone by and they still hadn't done much or had much fun yet caused young Jeremiah to express his desire NOT to leave the amusement park. "But we're having LOTS of fun!"

To which little Paul responded, "OH? We ARE? GOOD!"

At the end of the school year, the Blue-Bird (pre-Campfire) girls were having their annual Mothers Tea.

The Blue-Bird leader, a small lady with white hair, was giving a speech. "Now, girls," she said, "this summer you'll be taking lots of trips with your parents, and we must all remember not to litter."

When the girls just sort of sat there with kind of blank looks, the leader asked, "You DO know what LITTER means . . . don't you?"

With a doubtful look, one of the girls slowly raised her hand.

The leader asked, "Gail, do YOU know what litter means?"

Little seven-year-old Gail answered hesitantly, "I . . . think it has something to do with . . . puppies?"

Five-year-old J.D.'s response to the bank teller's compliment, "BOY! You sure are a CUTE little boy!" was: "I know it!"

Eighteen-year-old Valerie was packing her things prior to leaving for college. Her six-year-old sister, Judy, was helping (and visiting with) Valerie. It was close to the end of August and was very, very warm.

At last, after looking around the bedroom and not seeing anything more, Valerie closed and latched the last suitcase, then set it down by the door, commenting, "There! THAT should do it!"

Judy, however, brought over Valerie's robe, a long, extra-heavy winter robe.

"Aw-w, Judy," Valerie reasoned, "I don't need THAT!"

"Yes, you DO!" little Judy argued. "You never know WHEN you might get an obscene DOOR KNOCK!"

Eight-year-old Mike and his two young friends had been playing in the snow in a neighbor's yard.

Mike's father (a Pinehurst policeman) had very recently changed jobs.

"My dad has a new job, Harry . . . with an OFFICE in the county courthouse!" Mike proudly told his neighbor.

"What does your dad do, Mike?" Harry asked.

With some hesitation (and a puzzled look on his face), Mike answered, "He's a BASIN officer."

To which one of his young friends corrected "A PRO-bation officer."

Instantly, young Mike agreed, "YEAH! Yeah, THAT'S it . . . probation officer."

When Geri's older sister, Linda, was a little baby and cried at night, Mom would put Linda into bed with her and Dad.

Then, thirteen months later, baby Geri was born.

Dad's explicit orders to Mom were: "We are NOT going to put THIS baby in bed with us . . . no matter WHAT. . . . You are not bringing her into OUR bed! We already have ONE baby in here and that's enough!"

So . . . when baby Geri cried at night, Mom climbed into Geri's crib with her!

There was no Pepsi (other than a little bit of Mom's special Pepsi) on the shelves of the refrigerator in the kitchen, and the boys were thirsty.

Being too impatient to wait for his older brother, Benjamin, to bring some up (from the refrigerator in the basement) for the two of them, six-year-old Ricky decided NOT to wait . . . and, seeing Dad's luscious-looking ruby red grapefruit juice in front of him, Ricky poured himself a glassful, set the bottle on the cabinet, and started drinking (without tasting it first).

Upon his return into the kitchen with their Pepsi, Benjamin saw the almost empty bottle on the cabinet and the puckered-up face of his little brother. Grinning mischievously, Ben asked, "What's WRONG, Ricky?"

In a gasping sort of way, little Ricky replied, "My taste BUGS don't LIKE it!"

Listening to her mom and her boyfriend discussing the construction site accident where two pieces of heavy equipment (one of them a dozer) had dropped into the deep water of the Couer D'Alene lake along with a portion of the bank, Judy heard: "All of the men got out and no one got hurt, but the Cat is still down there."

Six-year-old Judy was horrified. "You mean all the men got out, and they left their poor cat in there to DROWN?!"

Two-year-old Ian was learning to talk. His words were clear, and he was very polite. If he wanted his older sister, Ellie, to give him a drink, it was: "Dink please, Ellie?" and: "Thank you." Or if he wanted something from Dad, it was: "Please, Daddy?" and: "Thank you." However, when he wanted something from Mom . . . it was: "Please, Daddy?" Mom corrected him with, "I'm MOMMY, thank you," and got: "You're welcome," from little Ian.

Riding with her mom and dad, four-year-old Sannette looked up at the old mine buildings up on the hillside above Pine Creek, Idaho, and asked, "What's THAT, Daddy?"

"THAT is a mine, Sannette," Dad started to explain.

"I didn't ask who OWNED it. . . . I asked what IS it!" little Sannette stated.

———————

A group of youngsters were discussing what it would be like when they got to Heaven.

"Do you think there will be cake in Heaven?" one of them asked, causing a little four-year-old boy to rationalize, "SURE! They have ANGEL food cake in HEAVEN!"

———————

From the floor, looking up at her mother (who was going through a basket of clean socks), four-year-old Betsy made the startling statement: "MOMMY! We have MCDONALD'S noses!"

———————

About his new stepdad, six-year-old Warren (asking for his three brothers as well as for himself), asked, "Mom, did Daddy marry us boys when you and him got married?"

———————

The little first-grade boy walked into the classroom, looked around, then told the teacher, "THIS is the room I'm going to be in!"

Looking at the little guy with his cute butch haircut standing there dressed in his knee-length pants, the teacher answered, "Marvelous! My name is Mrs. Allen . . . and what is YOUR name?"

While reaching down into his pocket, he said, "MY name is Nicholas . . . and just so you won't forget whom I am . . . " He slapped a nickel down on her desk!

Six-year-old Ricky had stubbed his toe, causing that toe's nail to start to come off.

A few days later, while soaking his foot, he asked, "Dad . . . do you think the TOE fairy will come?"

Aunt Esther and Uncle Tommy's golden wedding anniversary card had been received by the family. The card had a picture of the vibrant young couple fifty years ago (evidently very much in love) on one page and on the facing page a picture of the mature, happy couple today.

Looking at the card, while listening to her mother's warm and bubbly descriptive phrases of: "WONDERFUL!"; "BEAUTIFUL!"; AND "Such a GOOD idea!," a very serious seven-year-old Amanda decided, "Mom . . . I think Aunt Esther has SHRUNK!"

At the Pizza Plaza in Honolulu, Hawaii, Mom had ordered hot tea with lemon slices for herself. The three girls, fourteen-year-old Holly, her twelve-year-old sister, Leah, and their friend, thirteen-year-old Aubrey, placed their orders, and while waiting Leah decided to bet Aubrey that she (Leah) could keep a slice of lemon in her mouth longer than Aubrey could.

The bet was taken and each girl slipped a slice of lemon into her mouth.

Aubrey very quickly spits hers back out, but poor Leah had sunk her teeth into her juicy slice of lemon (in order to KEEP it in!).

Everyone sitting at the table was laughing, including Leah. The slice of lemon was STILL in her mouth, keeping her mouth wedged open in a continuous smile. Noting that Leah was also laughing spurred even more laughter from everyone at the table, and soon they were hysterical. Everyone in the place was looking at them.

Soon, tears were streaming from the eyes of the laughing Leah, and saliva was drooling down her chin. . . . That's right—she couldn't get the slice of lemon OUT! Her jaws were frozen, right from the FIRST bite!

Needless to say, Leah won the bet!

Due to his family living a good four hundred miles from Ian's maternal grandparent's home, as well as their work schedules, the family didn't get to visit very often. Now, the almost three-year-old Ian already seemed to be a pretty logical-thinking little guy and spoke very well for his age. The family had been using the maternal grandpa's car for a while, and little Ian was aware of this. "THIS is Grandpa's car?" Ian asked his dad.

"Yes, Ian, this is Grandpa's car."

"Where is Grandma's car?" Ian wanted to know.

Pointing to his own mother's car, Dad said, "THAT is Grandma's car."

Due to the earlier death of his paternal grandfather, little Ian never got to know him, causing the surprising question of: "What is a GRANDPA?"

Ah-h-h . . . CHICKEN for supper!

When asked which piece of chicken she wanted, three-and-a-half-year-old Sarah told her mother, "I wants the fly."

"WHAT?! You want the WHAT?" Mom asked incredulously.

Then, while holding her arms in a chicken wing–like way and flopping them up and down, little Sarah answered, "You know . . . the FLY!"

The bread was almost ready to be taken from the bread-maker and Great-Grandma was busy digging out the very hard frozen ice cream into Kyle's dish . . . so she asked Great-Grandpa, "Would you come in and take care of the bread, 'cause it's due to come out now."

When he took the loaf of hot bread out, he proceeded to brush melted butter on the top with a pastry brush.

Seeing this, eight-year-old Joey cried out in alarm, "GRANDMA! GRANDMA! GRANDMA . . . GRANDMA!"

"What's WRONG, Joey?" Great-Grandma asked.

"Grandpa is PAINTING the bread, Grandma!" young Joey exclaimed.

Eight-year-old Amanda had the chicken pox. It being a very severe case, the poor girl was REALLY covered and she was very, VERY uncomfortable.

In trying to console her daughter, Mom said, "Amanda, I understand from the old-timers THEY would relieve your terrible itch by giving you a soda bath."

"But, MOM . . . ," Amanda questioned, "look at all the POP you would need to go to the store and buy!"

Author's note: To a logger, a self-loader is a logging truck, equipped with a mechanical device that is a hydraulic boom, with a clam, making it possible for the truck driver to load a load of logs onto his own truck and trailer from the top of his truck, after which the driver wraps the load, then clamps the boom securely to the truck's subframe for the trip to the mill. After the logs are unloaded, the trailer is loaded onto the truck and the boom is then (again) secured to the subframe of the truck for the return trip to the woods for another load or home, whichever.

Joe's father had such a self-loading unit on his logging truck. As he liked the company of his young son (whenever possible) on his many trips, seven-year-old Joe was in the logging truck on a return trip via the freeway when something malfunctioned.

The boom rose (without Dad being aware) and it caught the bottom side of an overpass! The truck was nearly brought to an IMMEDIATE halt, with the boom on one side of the overpass and the truck reared on its back wheels (sort of resembling the Lone Ranger's reared stallion, Silver), the cab of the truck slightly touching the underside of the overpass. When the entire

163

self-loading unit broke loose from the truck (leaving the unit in the middle of the roadway), the truck instantly came back down on all wheels and young Joe was thrown to the floor of the cab. Picking himself up and climbing back into his seat, he calmly told his dad, "Gee, Dad . . . you need to be more careful. . . . You might get a TICKET!"

Three-year-old Sandra had just learned how to tie her shoes. Very proudly, she tied her shoes for Grandpa.

Grandpa (deciding to play the dumb bunny) stated, "Well . . . I'll BE! Can you do that AGAIN?"

So, the proud little Sandra tied her shoes again.

"Now . . . just HOW did you do THAT?" Grandpa asked in faked astonishment.

And Sandra tied her shoes AGAIN.

"I just don't see HOW you can do that . . . " Grandpa started to say, causing little Sandra to ask, "What am I going to have to DO . . . give you a DUMB-S-STRATION?!"

At Grandma's house, the almost three-year-old Bryson had been busy eating lots and lots of candy and cookies, causing Great-Grandma to exclaim, "My GOODNESS, Bryson! Where are you putting all of that? Do you have a hollow leg?!"

A very serious little Bryson leaned over and grabbed his leg with both hands and squeezed it . . . then looked up at his great-grandma to tell her, "No."

Fourteen-year-old Sandra was talking on the phone and doing her homework at the same time. Getting close to the bottom of the page, Sandra uttered an agonized, "OH NO!"

Her mother asked, "What's wrong, honey?"

"I'm almost DONE and I made a mistake, Mom! What am I going to do?"

"That's simple, Sandra. Just go in the other room, get your

Dad's white-out, rub it over the mistake, then redo the problem," her mother offered.

"I CAN'T!" Sandra wailed.

"Sure you can. It's in the other room and your dad won't mind . . . I'm sure."

"But I can't," Sandra insisted.

"Well, why NOT?" Mom wanted to know.

" 'Cause . . . I used it for SHOE polish!" the distraught teenager answered.

Five-year-old Ray was sitting in the pew of the Catholic church with his mother, listening to the priest delivering a long drawn out, solemn message in the quiet cathedral. All of a sudden, in a very, VERY loud voice, little Ray demanded to know, "WELL . . . when will this shindig be over? I want to go to the BOAT BASIN!"

Having visited his sister Daisy's fourth-grade classroom store and bought two pencils (and received NICE compliments from Daisy's teacher) one day, and the following day visiting another sister, Betsy's, kindergarten room (and also receiving NICE compliments from Betsy's teacher), the almost-three-year-old Ian decided that he LIKED school.

The following morning, little Ian was up, dressed (even had his jacket on!), and waited by the door after his older brothers and sisters left for school. Yes, Ian WANTED to go to school!

Mom explained, "No, WE have to stay home and clean house."

After a couple more requests (and denials) to go to school, Mom suggested that he help her in the kitchen. "Let's dump the trash, Ian." Then Mom proceeded to do just that.

Now, around their neighborhood there was a stray cat, and every time a door was open for a short time, this cat darted into the house to be met with a ringing order of, "Better throw that cat out!"

While Mom was putting a new trash bag into the wastebasket, little Ian and his baby sister, Annie, were on their hands and knees saying, "Meow . . . meow . . . "

"Do you know what I am, Mommy?" Ian asked.

"You are a kitty cat, Ian," Mom answered.

"Well . . . better throw ME out!" little Ian insisted.

The following conversation was overheard between the dentist and his young male patient in the Pinehurst, Idaho, Family Dentist office:

"I wish DENTISTS had never been invented!" the young boy exclaimed.

"Aw-w now," the patient dentist began, "you don't REALLY mean that, do you? Why . . . what would you do if you got an owwee in your tooth?"

After thinking about that for a short time, the little boy slowly drawled out, "I'd call a doctor!"

It seems that Grandma had gotten in trouble with D.J.'s mother for giving the three-year-old D.J. too many quarters to play the game machines with.

One evening at the café, little D.J. had already gone through his game-machine money and asked, "More quarters, Grandma?"

Grandma had to tell him, "No, D.J. Your mom has US on a limit."

"Aw-w . . . we won't ASK her!" little D.J. whispered quickly!

The Fircrest/Tacoma Washington, family owned and used a special pickup truck to haul leaves, limbs, and other refuse to the city dump, as well as building materials and other things when and where needed.

This special pickup truck has been special in different ways, as it has endeared itself to Dad and Mom by being there when needed, proving to be trustworthy even though it was old and an eyesore.

166

On one such trip home from the city dump, Dad and Mom with two sons, fourteen-year-old Jesse and twelve-year-old Benjamin, stopped by a 7-11 store. All four went inside with Dad taking the keys.

During the short time they were inside the store, someone tried to steal the pickup by hot-wiring it! However, the would-be thief was scared off before he accomplished his goal.

The family was discussing how close they had come to losing their pickup, which caused young Jesse to wonder, "Someone actually wanted to steal OUR pickup?" He asked in disbelief, "What would they want THIS for?!"

In the waiting room of the Seattle, Washington, hospital, a little three-year-old boy had been watching the man with his graying hair, mustache, and beard for quite some time. In fact, REALLY studying him.

Finally, the boy walked over to stand in front of the man. "You know what?" he asked. "When you grow up, YOU could be SANTA CLAUS!"

"You think so?" the man answered with a chuckle.

"YEAH! You kinda LOOK like him!"

The four sixteen-year-old Shoshone County, Idaho, friends (Pat, Donnie, Mike, and Neil) were out for a drive in Donnie's dad's new car when they stopped, giving a lift to two younger boys hitchhiking home to Wallace from a movie in Kellogg.

After the boys were settled in the car, the teenagers decided to have some fun. Trying to make the two boys believe they were desperate for money and just MAYBE looking for a bank to rob, they kept a continuous conversation going among themselves.

"Hey, Pat, you shouldn't have hit your grandma so HARD when you took her money. . . . You might have KILLED her, you know!" Neil chided.

"Yeah . . . but she shouldn't have hung on to that four dollars so TIGHT!" Pat answered gruffly.

"Yeah," Mike agreed. "Served her right! It's not enough. NOW we'll have to find a bank to rob!"

From behind the wheel, Donnie remarked, "Well, one thing's for sure—we're gonna need another car! THIS rattletrap ain't no good!"

In trying to keep on their good side, one of the hitchhikers offered, "Dr. Gnedniger has a new Cadillac—"

"Na-a-ah . . . we don't want THAT hunk of junk!" Donnie snarled.

The subject was dropped.

By this time, they were close to where the boys lived. As they were being let out of the car (and while the car door was still open) the comment: "HEY! I found my KNIFE!" was made in a surprised tone of voice, which made the boys depart quickly. As the boys split up, one boy leaped across the road, down the bank, and into the creek, and the other boy scrambled hastily up the hill on the other side of the road!

Donnie turned the car around, heading toward home with the teenagers laughing and discussing their "story." Neil was let out at his house in Kellogg, and the other three continued on to their homes in Smelterville and Pinehurst.

However, they didn't get very far before noticing a couple cars parked between Kellogg and Smelterville. . . .

Before they knew it, they were pulled over and immediately surrounded by nine police cars! Some of the officers were armed with submachine guns and pulled the boys from the car, ordering, "Stand with your hands on the car!"

They were searched, handcuffed, and taken to the county jail in Wallace where they were put in a lineup, and one of the (two) hitchhikers, pointing his shaking finger at Pat, nervously exclaimed, "THAT'S one of them! I'll NEVER forget THAT face!"

Yes, due to their witty creativeness (and good acting ability), three of the four teenagers spent part of the night incarcerated, as it wasn't until a deputy sheriff (a friend of Pat's dad) recognized two of the teenagers that their parents were called (in the wee hours of the morning) to "come get them and take them home!" A lengthy discussion was held, after which the boys nearly lost their driving privileges for one year.

With all of the complications caused by their dumb act (they hadn't THOUGHT about the hitchhikers calling the police!), the young men decided their "funny story" wasn't so funny, after all.

But the group certainly was famous (or IN-famous?) at school for a while!

THAT'S ALL, FOLKS!